TEXTS

THE ESSENTIAL GUIDE TO CONTEMPORARY LITERATURE

Toni Morrison

11/03

Also available in Vintage Living Texts

Martin Amis

Margaret Atwood

Louis de Bernières

Sebastian Faulks

Ian McEwan

Salman Rushdie

Jeanette Winterson

VINTAGE
LIVING
TEXTS

Toni Morrison

THE ESSENTIAL GUIDE
TO CONTEMPORARY
LITERATURE

Beloved

Jazz

Paradise

VINTAGE

Published by Vintage 2003

2 4 6 8 10 9 7 5 3 1

Copyright © Jonathan Noakes and Margaret Reynolds 2002

The right of Jonathan Noakes and Margaret Reynolds to be identified
as the authors of this work has been asserted by them in accordance with
the Copyright, Designs and Patents Act, 1988.

First published in Great Britain in 2003 by Vintage
Random House, 20 Vauxhall Bridge Road,
London SW1V 2SA

Random House Australia (Pty) Limited
20 Alfred Street, Milsons Point, Sydney,
New South Wales 2061, Australia

Random House New Zealand Limited
18 Poland Road, Glenfield,
Auckland 10, New Zealand

Random House (Pty) Limited
Endulini, 5A Jubilee Road, Parktown 2193, South Africa

The Random House Group Limited Reg. No. 954009
www.randomhouse.co.uk

A CIP catalogue record for this book is available from the British Library

ISBN 009943766X

Papers used by Random House are natural, recyclable products made
from wood grown in sustainable forests; the manufacturing processes
conform to the environmental regulations of the country of origin.

Typeset by Palimpsest Book Production Limited, Polmont, Stirlingshire

Printed and bound in Great Britain by
Bookmarque Ltd, Croydon, Surrey

CONTENTS

Paradise

VINTAGE LIVING TEXTS: REFERENCE

Acknowledgements

We owe grateful thanks to all at Random House. Most of all our debt is to Caroline Michel and her team at Vintage – especially Marcella Edwards, Ali Reynolds, Jason Arthur and Liz Foley – who have given us generous and unfailing support. Thanks also to Philippa Brewster and Georgina Capel, Michael Meredith, Angela Leighton, Harriet Marland, Louisa Joyner, to all our colleagues, and to our partners and families. We would also like to thank the teachers and students at schools and colleges around the country who have taken part in our trialling process, and who have responded so readily and warmly to our requests for advice. And finally, our thanks to Toni Morrison for her work without whom . . . without which . . .

VINTAGE LIVING TEXTS

Preface

About this series

Vintage Living Texts: The Essential Guide to Contemporary Literature is a new concept in reading guides. Our aim is to provide readers of all kinds with an intelligent and accessible introduction to key works of contemporary literature. Each guide suggests techniques for reading important contemporary novels, and offers a variety of back-up materials that will give you ways into the text – without ever telling you what to think.

Content

All the books reproduce an extensive interview with the author, conducted exclusively for this series. This is not to say that we believe that the author's word is law. Of course it isn't. Once his or her book has gone out into the world he or she becomes simply yet another – if singularly competent – reader. This series recognises that an author's contribution may be valuable, and intriguing, but it puts the reader in control.

Every title in the series is author-focused and covers at

least three of their novels, along with relevant biographical, bibliographical, contextual and comparative material.

How to use this series

In the reading activities that make up the core of each guide you will see that you are asked to do two things. One comes from the text; that is, we suggest what you should focus on, whether it's a theme, the language or the narrative method. The other concentrates on your own response. We want you to think about how you are reading and what skills you are bringing to bear in doing that reading. So this part is very much about you, the reader.

The point is that there are many ways of responding to a text. You could concentrate on the methods you might use to compare this text with others. In that case, look for the sections headed 'Compare'. Or you might want to do something more individual, and analyse how you are reacting to a text and what it means to you, in which case, pick out the approaches labelled 'Imagine' or 'Ask Yourself'.

Of course, it may well be that you are reading these texts for an examination. In that case you will have to go for the more traditional methods of literary criticism and look for the responses that tell you to 'Discuss' or 'Analyse'. Whichever level you (or your students) are at, you will find that there is something here for everyone. However, we're not suggesting that you stick solely to the approaches we offer, or that you tackle all of the exercises laid out here. Choose whatever most interests you, or whatever best suits your purposes.

Who are these books for?

Students will find that these guides are like a good teacher. They introduce the life and work of the author, set each novel in its context, explain key ideas and literary critical terms as they arise, suggest comparative exercises in a number of media, and ask focused questions to encourage a well-informed, analytical approach to reading the novels in a way that is rigorous, but still entertaining.

Teachers will find in this series a rich source of ideas for teaching contemporary novels and their contexts, particularly at AS, A and undergraduate levels. The exercises on each text have been tailored to meet the various assessment objectives laid down in the subject criteria for GCE AS and GCE A Level English Literature, and are explained in such a way that they can easily be selected and fitted into a lesson plan. Given the diversity of ways in which the awarding bodies have devised their specifications to meet these assessment objectives, a wide range of exercises is offered. We've had fun devising the plans, and we hope they'll be fun for you when you come to teach and learn with them.

And if you are neither a teacher nor a student of contemporary literature, but someone reading for your own pleasure? Well, if you've ever wanted someone to introduce you to a novelist's work in a way that will let you trust your own judgement and read more confidently, then this guide is also for you.

Whoever you are, we hope that you will enjoy using these books and that they will send you back to the novels to find new pleasures.

All page numbers in this text refer to the Vintage editions.

Toni Morrison

Introduction

Toni Morrison thinks in colour. In the interview which follows she describes how she contrived to bleach the opening of her novel *Beloved*. Sethe lives with her mother-in-law and daughter in 'the gray and white house on Bluestone Road'. The stairs are white, leading to a blue and white second floor, 'discreet flecks of yellow sprinkled among a blizzard of snowdrops all backed by blue', and the season is bleak: 'Winter in Ohio is especially rough if you had an appetite for color'. All is colourless, sepia, and into this drained world comes the orange patch on the quilt, Baby Suggs craving 'Bring a little lavender in, if you got any. Pink, if you don't', Paul D. with his 'peachstone skin' stepping into 'a pool of red and undulating light that locked him where he stood'. The intrusion of colour is, says Morrison, 'wild', 'like a gunshot', 'momentous' and with a 'heavy, theatrical quality'. It is, she says, all to do with 'palette'.

Toni Morrison is a great writer. Critical opinion has tried hard to label her work, but she escapes definition all the time. Only one thing is certain. That reading one of Morrison's novels is a whole experience. It includes everything, every aspect of sensation and experience, every imaginative effort and every constructive effort of will to follow her thread, to listen to her music, to feel her characters' feelings, to see her colours. When we interviewed Morrison for this book we asked her about her reaction to one critic's description of her work as 'synaesthetic'. She had not heard this term applied to her writing. We knew it was right, simply because that total and delicate attention to sensation in the imagination was our own experience of reading her books.

Morrison's works demand an honesty from readers. Her work is always open, as her imagination is always open, ready for re-examination, and open to taking risks. 'Writing', Morrison has said, 'is about danger for me; it's like life – you can go under.' There is a solid connection between personal life and the act of writing. Morrison is unusual for a writer of fiction in that she is conscious of, and has had extensive experience of, the two sides of the writing process that flank the actual work itself. She knows about the practical and business side of bringing fiction into the world because she worked, for many years, as a senior editor for Random House publishers. She knows about how fiction is received in the wider world, because she is an academic and critic and teaches at the University of Princeton in New Jersey, USA. Every aspect of the process has been scrutinised and interrogated by Morrison, and always with the same openness to risk and to feeling.

From her first book onward, Morrison took risks. In *The Bluest Eye* (1970) form was matched to subject matter. Pecola Breedlove – growing up in 1940's Ohio, poor, abused, raped, disregarded for reasons of class, race, sex – finds that she cannot reconcile what the institutionalised and 'official' stories tell, or what conventional reading tells, with the facts of her own degraded experience. The text has to convey this crucial split, so the narrative comes across broken, fragmented, full of hints and suggestions, pulling different ways.

Reviewers and critics tried to place Morrison. Because of her subject matter she was proclaimed a black writer, an Afro-American writer, a woman writer. Because of her choice of settings she was named an Americanist inheriting the questions examined by William Faulkner or Ernest Hemingway. Because of her style she was a Modernist working with experimental form. Because she exploited the marvellous and the supernatural she was a magical realist.

In fact, Morrison is nothing but herself. Her works are unique. What they have in common is that they are 'Morrisonian'. 'I refuse to let them off the hook', she said in 1988, 'about whether I'm a Black woman writer or not, I'm under a lot of pressure to become something else. That is why there is so much discussion of how my work is influenced by other "real" writers, for example white Southern writers whom I'm constantly compared to.'

Strangely enough, the moment when Morrison might be most obviously incorporated, is also the moment when her special, particular qualities may be most recognisable. In 1987 Morrison published *Beloved* which won the Pulitzer Prize for fiction, the Robert F. Kennedy Award and the Elizabeth Cady Stanton Award from the Organization for Women. In 1989 she was awarded the Nobel Prize for Literature. The prizes paradoxically legitimise the work, and yet acknowledge its special outsideness, its unlikeness to anything else.

In some ways Morrison's true subject is something that is not said, or rather that can often only be uttered in the spaces in between what is spoken. The story of *Beloved* is the story of a haunting. There is a ghost, and there is a true history of suffering, there is a renegotiated past living on in memory, and there is a present. Some of these layers are actual, some of them live only in the minds of the characters – and, of course, in the minds of the readers. But they are all real. The actual lived life is not privileged over the imaginative life. They exist side by side, inextricably woven, intertwined. With this method what cannot be said can always be implied. We become rich through an enhanced method of storytelling.

This is a passage from *Beloved* (p. 58).

'Where your diamonds?' Beloved searched Sethe's face.

'Diamonds? What would I be doing with diamonds?'

'On your ears.'

'Wish I did. I had some crystal once. A present from a lady I worked for.'

'Tell me', said Beloved, smiling a wide happy smile. 'Tell me your diamonds.'

It became a way to feed her. Just as Denver discovered and relied on the delightful effect sweet things had on Beloved, Sethe learned the profound satisfaction Beloved got from storytelling. It amazed Sethe (as much as it pleased Beloved) because every mention of her past life hurt. Everything in it was painful or lost. She and Baby Suggs had agreed without saying so that it was unspeakable; to Denver's enquiries Sethe gave short replies or rambling incomplete reveries. Even with Paul D., who had shared some of it and to whom she could talk with at least a measure of calm, the hurt was always there – like a tender place in the corner of her mouth that the bit left.

But, as she began telling about the earrings, she found herself wanting to, liking it. Perhaps it was Beloved's distance from the event itself, or her thirst for hearing it – in any case it was an unexpected pleasure.

Beloved does not exist, but Sethe 'feeds' her, she 'thirsts', she consumes 'sweet things'. The earrings aren't present, though there were some once, and they weren't diamonds. Sethe – because she is speaking to no one, or only to a ghost – is not speaking at all. She is still not uttering the pain and loss which live within her memory. Yet – out of all these negatives come three positives. In Morrison's narrative Sethe's story is *told*, the unacknowledged 'unspeakable' gets spoken, and there is 'pleasure' in it, and the telling is rich as 'diamonds'.

When her prose is broken down like this it's clear that, on the one hand, Morrison demands a tremendous imaginative effort from her readers. But on the other hand her approach is so powerful, that the readers do not even notice it. This is what makes Morrison a great storyteller; her readers are simply seduced by the telling. It's also what makes Morrison a great prose stylist as the simple implied oral tale is couched in words and images that convey its fullness to us without becoming too contrived or drawing too much attention to the words themselves. Morrison's wish is to make the story appear oral, meandering, effortless, spoken – to have the reader feel the narrator without identifying that narrator, and encouraging the reader to work with the author in constructing the book. What is left out is as important as what is there.

With her layering method, Morrison tells many stories that aren't there: the lost stories of slavery, imprisonment, displacement and torture; the hidden stories of rape and the deaths of children and of women's loss; the secret stories of abuse, degradation, and the theft of identity. And yet of course, hidden, secret, lost though they may be, those stories are real and they are true.

By mixing time, magic and imagination, by blending the everyday and the phantasmagoric, by letting words say so much more than they mean, Morrison tells us much more than we know. We have to listen as she listens so that we can attend to her music and hear her voices. In the interview (pp. 19–20) Morrison says that her 'surefire' method of testing her fiction is by talking to her characters and asking them: 'is this really what it was like for you?' or, 'would you have said this?'. This is something that Morrison has said before: 'My audience is always the people in the book I am writing at the time, I don't think of an external audience.'

This is another paradox. Morrison addresses herself to, and listens to, fictions which do not exist. But in doing so she appeals to us, her readers. If we attend, if we care, we will see her rhythm, hear her vision, feel her colours.

Interview with Toni Morrison

New York: 1 November 2002

MR: I'd like to begin by asking you about storytelling methods. What do stories consist of as far as you're concerned? Is it more important to you to represent an authentic story, a first person story, an oral story, rather than an official history?

TM: I want to scour the official history for the alternate history that exists, sometimes parallel to it, more often underneath it. It gleams through the official story in curious ways – a shot here, a facet there – and it's the kind of thing you want to pursue, and when you cannot find all of the data, you have to imagine it. But I don't want the story, the alternate, or the underneath or repressed story, told in a manner that duplicates the official narrative. I want the speakers, the characters, to assume whatever format they wish. Sometimes it's their thoughts, sometimes it's a fugue, sometimes it's just incredible kinds of silence. For example, in *Paradise* – I remember reading a newspaper ad in the mid nineteenth century for black people, ex and former slaves to emigrate to the West. And they were setting up all-black towns. That movement was fairly well known among historians, but what was interesting to me was one of the columns that appeared in one of the most popular black newspapers which said 'Come prepared or not at all'. It struck me that there was a kind of exclusivity and rejection even among those who themselves had been fleeing from a certain kind of rejection. So it was the story underneath the emigrant story that I was interested in.

MR: In a way this relates to many of your other themes to do with memory and haunting and misremembering. Why are you so anxious about the volatility of memory – the unknownness of what we think we know?

TM: There is an enormous amount of hypocrisy, an enormous amount of secrecy and deliberate erasure of the cultural narrative in the United States. On the one hand there's this myth of 'all are welcome, all are free, all have opportunity', and the reality is quite different – which is not to say that there is not success or promise. All nations build their own mythologies in order to swagger or get along in the world. This country has a lot of buried histories. It's not unusual that they project a certain story or narrative in order to cut a certain kind of figure, but it leaves many of us with a superficial knowledge, even a superficial life, if we don't really understand more of the truth, but more particularly if we don't hear the voices of the people who lived through certain periods or within them without sanction, without notice, and without real support. Until the pasts – the various pasts, because there are more than one – surface, it just seems to me that the whole temper as well as the colour and the depth and the richness of the culture can never be formed.

MR: That relates to the question of identity which is something that you focus on a great deal, in *Beloved* particularly. How people can create themselves – is that an issue that you see going on in your novels?

TM: Creating themselves? In large part, or *discovering* themselves. You know, if you think that your whole identity is your race, because for the larger population that *is* your identity, then somehow you narrow yourself down, or you can narrow yourself down into simply being a black girl, or a black woman, and that's all you are and all you do, although life contradicts you at every moment. So the complexity and the broadening of identity, rather than the narrowing of it is much more my focus. The fact that the characters are black people leads people to assume that I am merely interested in what black people think and do and how they behave under duress, or not. What I am primarily interested in is how complicated identity is, and that if it is restricted, or hampered by one or two definitions – gender, or race, or class, or any of the large things – then you are forced to respond, or you become forced to respond, in three areas, while your real living life, of memory, of other people's stories, of experience, is lost. Living life is reduced to nothing, and that's what the richness of a human being's life truly is.

MR: There's a line at the end of *Beloved* that always strikes me: 'Everybody knew what she was called, but nobody anywhere knew her name'. Does that suggest that kind of freedom, independence, multiplicity of naming and identity?

TM: Yes, very much so. In addition to which, the naming thing is a critical thing in African American culture because of the loss of names, the loss of tribal names, African names. A great deal of drama surrounds the choice of names that were given to slaves, a great deal of drama surrounds the rejection of a slave name, even to the point, you may remember, of groups of people calling themselves 'X'. Also, it's a very personal thing: what your name is, who gave it to you, what it means. Then there's the fondness for nicknames, or for derogatory names, within the culture, as a way of forcing you to confront your vulnerabilities right away, in order to strengthen you for life. You know, calling Louis Armstrong 'Satchmo' meaning 'satchel mouth'. Making fun of one another in nicknames, has a cruelty to it, but also a kind of necessary 'girding up thy loins', so to speak, for what might be down the road.

MR: You're always intrigued with the many meanings of words, aren't you? I was thinking about the end of *Beloved*: 'This is not a story to pass on'. Well, there are two puns in there, but then I thought, there's a third pun – it's not a story to pass on to somebody else, it's not a story to 'pass on' as in 'to miss out on', but also it's not a story to pass on, as in 'passing' – as in, the whole question of Passing as white in society.

TM: [She laughs.] True. The dusting off of these very ordinary expressions and words is a great part of the delight I take in writing. Lots of people think my prose is rich, meaning 'ornate'. And it's just the opposite of that. It is – I think – very lean and understated. But it does two things I hope: one is to use resonances that alter definitions of ordinary words, and at the same time, make room for readers to bring in their own complicated emotions to the text. And I think it's their complicated response that might lead them to think that it's in the writing. I remember *Sula*, in which a girl seems to be watching passively while her mother burns, and, later on, her grandmother thinks that she was not 'paralysed', but that she was 'interested'. Now that word, 'interested', is probably like 'nice'. It has no meaning, it has no weight. It's what you say when you have nothing to say: 'oh it was interesting', 'he's very interesting'. Under those circumstances, the original power of a very ordinary word – when you find a girl watching her mother burn – and you say she was 'interested': that has I think the same sort of aura and layer of meaning that the example that you just gave about 'pass on'.

MR: Though you say that you feel that your writing is simple and not ornate, you do use a musical analogy. I'm thinking of *Jazz* especially, but a bit earlier on you said something about using a 'fugue'. So is music as a form something that you exploit in writing?

TM: The music is inherent in the structure, in repetition and crescendos, not in the choice of words. I wanted very much in *Jazz* to catch the feeling of riffs, of staccato, of lyricism, of blues. But that would be in the organisation of the sentence, the selection of words, but not in so-called high brow or extraliterary words, because I don't want to do that. I'm delighted and fascinated by nuance in language. So much of street language and colloquial language and the parlance of these people was oral – the language of ordinary people in African-American culture – so that my tendency would be to try to shape it so that you could actually almost have a sound. The text has to work quietly, I think, on the page, but it ought to have a sound as well. *Beloved* was kind of sermonic – it had a build, *Beloved* did, that was not secular. Whereas *Jazz* is very secular, and very 'Jazz' – you know, sensual, risky, a little bit dangerous.

MR: Your work has been described as offering 'synaesthetic' prose – including every kind of sensation. Is that a description that you would buy?

TM: Oh . . . well that's good. That's a good thing. I hadn't heard that. I'm pleased.

MR: Well, yes. It's got sounds and colours, feelings and smells, all of that kind of richness.

TM: It's interesting to me – when you describe these various kinds of sensations – you know a lot of it is *palette*, the placing of colour in the text. Or the withdrawing of colour. As in *Beloved*, for example, where everything is sort of colourless, sepia, I saw that bleached canvas. So that when colour appears, it's wild. The orange patch on the quilt is like a gunshot. The woman is lying in bed thinking of colour, just dreaming of it. Sethe, when she finally falls in love, or thinks she is going to have a mate, suddenly the world takes on colour. But normally the colour is withdrawn, for that reason. So that when it does appear, then it has a momentous, heavy, theatrical quality. Whereas in *Song of Solomon* I was introducing red, white, and blue in the opening of snow, and red velvet, and blue wings – for no particular reason, not to communicate anything particular to the reader, but because I do see the scene and the colour is a part of it, as well as the language. It's a merging of the visual and the linguistic for me.

MR: I set myself a little task, and I just looked at the first three lines of the first three chapters of *Paradise*: 'They shoot the white girl first'; 'The neighbours seemed pleased when the babies smothered'; 'Either the pavement was burning or she had sapphires hidden in her shoes'. I began to see a sort of parallel thing of beauty and horror, simplicity and exaggeration, always this doubleness.

TM: Yeah, my son told me that the other day – it was an accusation – that I made terrible things too beautiful. That I should maybe stop that and just make terrible things terrible. Well, he's a painter and a musician. They see things differently. I just want to make it accessible and original, so that you think, something that you know could happen to anybody, so that you feel it and see it for the first time. There's a way in which a woman walks in high heeled shoes, and there are twelve ways to say that, all twelve of which have been said. But if she's sort of switching and tipping a little bit, it may look as though she had a pebble in her shoe, but that would suggest pain, so, since she didn't take it out, it must be sapphires or diamonds or something. So it's to try to give the visual quality and associate this little tart with luxury and jewellery and sexuality and so on.

MR: In *Jazz* especially, but certainly in other works too, there is the idea of the city, the multitudes, many different places. What kind of freedoms does the image of the city give you?

TM: Well, it forces me into a certain area of research that I dread, but I do have to go there if I'm going to – as I frequently do – impose either the divine, or the dream, or the supernatural into the narrative, then the places have to be very realistic. You have to anchor them. Otherwise the fantasy or the supernatural or the dreamlike qualities don't work, if everything is floating about and nothing is nailed down. So, I try to have streets and towns and neighbourhoods, geography exactly the way it is or would be. For example, how long a street is; I draw maps of everything and plans of the house. Or I go places and see what they look like. And then, when I am talking about women who have no navels, or ghosts that appear out of the water, or what have you, it's in a particular place, and therefore you're anchored and you can be as imaginative as you like. Provided you have the accuracy and the legitimacy and the authenticity of place.

MR: With *Beloved*, *Jazz* and *Paradise*, these three books go together, so that there is a re-working of ideas and themes, again, in a kind of multiple way. Are you conscious of returning to things that you've already done and re-visiting areas to re-think them?

TM: Well, no, not till after I've finished, and then I say 'Oh, this was an extension of one thing or another'.

MR: So you become your own reader?

TM: I did know that, starting with *Beloved*, I was really writing about the way in which women love things – the kinds of female love there are: love of children, and displacement, how one can displace love of self for love of something else. And it's one of the virtues, I think, that women have – also one of the dangers. You know, you can overdo it all. And the second one was romantic love, and I didn't really know where I was going to go from there, and then I realised that one of the main ignitions of the movement of black people west, one of the reasons they were able to survive, was their faith. So that, in a sense, the third book was another kind of love, although not limited to women, which was love of God. I wanted women, or at least some of the women, to be *true* believers, not fakes or phonies, but people who had a very intimate rela-tionship with their God or their spirits, whether it was in the convent with that woman Connie, or whether it was people in the town, which drove much of their imaginative life as well as their social and political life.

MR: In the Afterword for [the Vintage edition of] *The Bluest Eye*, there's a fascinating bit where you talked about the tech-nique you used of 'breaking the narrative into parts that had to be re-assembled by the reader'. How much work do you expect your readers to do?

TM: Oh, as much as I! Well, not actual writing. But that's the way I read, it's the way I think readers who love books read. Which is, carefully and not unwilling to read them again, and not unwilling to find something that you hadn't seen before. Or sometimes it's just really taking a little side step down an alleyway you didn't even know was there. It's writing a story that can be enjoyed by people who are not fastidious readers, but to have the real story available to those who are very fastidious readers, and to have that pleasure of revelation – of something seen, or heard, or touched – in the language, that sometimes you get, frequently you get, in poetry. But the kinds of novels that I like to read are the classic ones, the ones where you can always go back and look at it from a different point of view again, or see something that you haven't before. I don't think that's *work*. I think that's what it's really about. We accept that with music very easily. With good music, we can hear it over and over again, and it means something different ten years later. You hear a song when you're sixteen, and then when you're twenty-six you hear the same song and it's a different song. The song isn't different: you're different. Then other things happen and when you hear the same song later it's different again. Reading, and all arts really, have that for me, whether it's dance or painting or music, but certainly it's very very much a part of the thrill, the sheer delight of reading.

MR: Do you have an ideal reader? Or is it just somebody who's delighted by reading?

TM: I don't have an idea of a reader. I sometimes think I'm it. But sometimes I have trouble in persuading myself that this is well done, or honest even. Sometimes you get caught up in your 'beauty' thing and looking for it. [She laughs.] And then you forget what you're working towards. But I have a fairly sure-fire test. I conjure up the characters in the book, and I sort of ask them – 'is this really what it was like for you?' or, 'would you have said this?', or what have you. And it's one of a little bag of tricks that I'm sure each author has, in order to keep yourself on the mark.

Trilogy

AN INTRODUCTION

The three texts focused on here form a trilogy. So, as well as considering contexts for each individual novel, think about the collection as one entire text.

Focus on: the number three

RESEARCH AND CONSIDER . . .

— What is a trilogy? Look at Morrison's comments on the trilogy on pp. 17–18.

— Where else is a grouping of three important? For example, in Christian thought, what is the Holy Trinity? Heaven, Earth and Hell, as well as Heaven, Purgatory and Hell, form important threes.

— How do these meanings influence your reading of the texts? For instance, you may have focused on the relationship of the number three to Christianity and the Holy Trinity: God the Father, God the Son and God the Holy Spirit. How do you interpret these roles in relation to *Beloved, Jazz* and *Paradise*?

As you read, look out for groupings of three in the text. If you divide the characters into groups of three, what patterns do you come up with? Who complicates the situation between three characters?

Focus on: death

COMPARE . . .

The theme of death, and the trauma experienced by the bereaved is central to the three novels. Whether it is Beloved's death, Dorcas's murder, or the attack upon the Convent in *Paradise*, the novels revolve around central absences; characters may reinhabit the tales (like Beloved's ghost, and Dorcas's memory), but the fact of death is itself central. Your detailed analysis of the texts will look at death in many different ways under headings such as:

- Grief
- Remembrance
- Violence
- Ghosts
- Absence.

Or with reference to specific characters, such as:

- Beloved
- Dorcas
- Save-Marie.

— Think about Morrison's central engagement with death in terms of these varying focuses. Look at its presentation as trauma in the minds of the survivors, and compare the different cultural versions of what it may mean.

Focus on: religion

COMBINE . . .

As you work your way through the novels you will become aware of the role of religion in the various texts. Perhaps it is most clearly highlighted in *Paradise*, but Violet's attempt to stab Dorcas at her funeral in *Jazz*, and Sethe's naming of Beloved – because it refers to the opening words of the funeral service – in *Beloved*, provide examples of the central importance of Christian ideals to the trilogy.

— Combine your research and knowledge of the novels' treatment of religion to think about how it circumscribes the trilogy as a whole.

Focus on: the idea of motherhood

RELATE . . .

— The idea of the role of the mother is important in each of the three novels. Think about its treatment in relation to the central characters. Consider the concepts of being a mother as they are teased out differently in each of the texts.

— Relate the specific discussions of your conception of 'motherhood' to how Morrison complicates it in her characterisations of Mavis, Violet and Sethe. Could you argue that the three novels are bound to one another in their collapse of the 'anti-maternal'? How is Morrison centrally concerned with breaking down that binary opposition for and against the idealised 'mother'?

Focus on: inscription

BEAR IN MIND . . .

— As you look at the language and tone of the novels explore the idea of writing itself. Think of its historical importance – illiteracy is a key weapon in the oppression of under-privileged groups in society, denying them a public voice. This debate appears in all three novels, look at Morrison's comments in the interview on pp. 11–12 and on p. 15.

— Bear in mind the exercises that focus on:

- Forms of writing
- Oral versus written narratives
- The authority of the narrative voice
- Arguments about linguistic meaning.

— Link these together in order to consider the trilogy's interrogation of the idea of inscribing words with meaning.

VINTAGE
LIVING
TEXTS

Beloved

IN CLOSE-UP

Reading guides for

BELOVED

BEFORE YOU BEGIN TO READ . . .
— Read the interview with Morrison. You will see that she identifies a number of themes:

- Stories – written versus oral
- History
- Origins
- Naming
- Memory.

Other themes that it may be useful to consider while reading the novel include:

- Absence and hauntings
- The history of slavery
- Ownership.

While you are reading *Beloved*, *Jazz* and *Paradise* in detail, it is worth bearing these overall themes in mind. At the end of the detailed reading activities you will find suggested contexts, which will help you to situate the themes in a wider framework.

The reading activities given below are designed to be used imaginatively. Choose whichever sections most interest you or are most useful for your own purposes. Some sections are linked, as themes are highlighted at different points in the novel, but again choose whether or not you want to look at one specific instance or trace the theme throughout the novel.

Reading activities: detailed analysis

PART ONE
SECTION I (pp. 3–9)

Focus on: openings

LIST . . .
— Paying attention only to the opening paragraph, draw up a list of the information you are given here. What do you learn about plot and characterisation in these opening sentences? You might find it useful to make a family tree from the information provided in this opening section, to refer back to throughout your analysis of the novel.

CONSIDER . . .
— Look over the information you have distilled from pp. 3–9. Why does Morrison give you this information at the outset? What category would you choose for the 'facts' you are given here:

● Biography?
● History?
● Story?
● Myth?
● Horror?
● Memoir?

— Pick a term and write down the reasons for your choice. Which category do you think is privileged here? Work through the section picking out textual evidence for your choice. You might like to come back to this question as you progress through the novel. Does your choice differ depending upon the point you are focusing on in the text? What term do you come to when you have considered this question at the end of the novel?

COMPARE AND DISCUSS . . .

— If you are in a class, get into groups and evaluate your choices. Look particularly at the reasons you have given for your choices. Do they overlap? Debate which is the most appropriate term, paying particular attention to the reasons you have listed for your choices.

Focus on: the theme of dead/alive

EVALUATE . . .

> 'We could move,' she suggested once to her mother-in-law.
>
> 'What'd be the point?' asked Baby Suggs. 'Not a house in the country ain't packed to its rafters with some dead Negro's grief.' (p. 5)

— The relationship between 'dead' and 'alive' characters in *Beloved* is extremely complex. Work your way through this opening section thinking about how the relationship between the dead and the living is established. For example, how does Paul D react to what he feels at 124? How do Denver and Sethe physically manage the spirits they encounter? How are the spirits described, in natural or physical terms?

PART ONE
SECTION 2 (pp. 9–19)

Focus on: the theme of 'Sweet Home'

DETAIL . . .

— Look at the history of 'Sweet Home' on pp. 9–11. How does Morrison ironise the idea of a 'Sweet Home'? Put together the terms you associate with 'home' and then reread Paul's recollections of the Kentucky farm. How do they undermine or oppose your ideas of what makes up a home?

NOTE AND EXPLORE . . .

— In this section you are given the slave history of the characters you meet in *Beloved*. The novel returns again and again to events at Sweet Home. When you encounter these passages, think about and note down how Morrison uses the example of Sweet Home to discuss the evils of slavery. What examples of its cruelty are you given in this section?

— Expand upon these notes as you read further into the novel. Use them as a basis for thinking about the 'Institution of Slavery' in America, both within the text and in terms of its context.

Focus on: the theme of naming

EXAMINE . . .

— Sethe describes the scars on her back as a tree because 'That's what [the white girl] called it' (p. 16). Examine Paul D's reaction to the 'tree' in this section. How is the 'scar' turned into something positive here through its naming?

COMPARE AND CONTRAST . . .

— Go back to the opening section of the text and compare Sethe's description of how 'Beloved' came to be named (pp. 4–5) with the description of the 'tree'. How do these two examples illustrate the importance of naming? What consequences for naming are suggested here?

— This, again, is a theme to which the text returns, but at this point you might like to jot down some ideas about characters' names, such as 'Baby Suggs' and 'Denver', to come back to when you have developed your textual analysis.

Focus on: the theme of ghosts

CONSIDER . . .

— Look primarily at the end of the section (pp. 18–19). How does the text suggest that the physical movement of the house is supernatural? Look closely at the language – for example, the use of 'she' and 'it'. How is the link made to Sethe's dead baby 'Beloved'?

EXPAND . . .

— What expectations does the introduction of the ghost, at this point, set up for the reader? Be specific about what you expect to occur and what you think the consequences will be. (This exercise is useful even if this is not your first reading of *Beloved*, as long as you pay close attention to the passage referred to here. What, specifically, is suggested *here*?)

RECONSIDER . . .

— Come back to this set of expectations at the end of the novel and compare them to your fuller textual discussion. Does the novel meet your expectations? In what ways have they been challenged?

PART ONE
SECTION 3 (pp. 20–7)

Focus on: the theme of intimacy

EVALUATE . . .

— Looking closely at the language on pp. 20–21 and p. 24, consider the nature of Sethe and Paul D's sexual encounter. Which clauses highlight the lack of closeness here?

— Which metaphor does Morrison use to suggest that this encounter lacks the intimacy the pair desire? How is it extended to indicate the lack of emotional as well as sexual closeness between the two?

CONTRAST . . .

— Now look at the stories that Paul D considers in between the sexual encounters (pp. 21–4, 25–8). How do these contrast with the lack of sexual and emotional intimacy between Sethe and Paul D? Again, pick out particular examples or phrases, or specific stories. For example, look at the two journeys: Sixo's to meet the Thirty-Mile Woman, and Paul D's to meet Sethe.

LINK . . .

— Think about Sethe's memories at the end of this section (pp. 26–7). How are the contrasted stories linked in a discussion of intimacy in this story? Do some stories offer explanations for the others? For instance, do the past examples explain the current lack of closeness? Think about the common themes in the different stories of this section. What impression of 'intimacy' is left upon the reader in this section?

PART ONE
SECTION 4 (pp. 28–38)

Focus on: language and tone

DETAIL . . .

— How does the description alter to suggest 'magic', or something spiritual, in the paragraphs that frame this section (pp. 28–9, 37–8)?

EXTEND . . .

— How does Denver's 'magic' space separate her from the other characters here? Think both about the location and the effect that the text suggests it has upon her.

Focus on: the theme of memory and 'rememory'

DISTINGUISH . . .

— Examine Denver's version of her birth (pp. 29–35). How is this different from a standard reflection of Sethe's? Pick out the incidents that make this an unusual account of a memory.

— Think about this story in relation to Sethe's assertion 'If a house burns down, it's gone, but the place – the picture of it – stays, and not just in my rememory, but out there [. . .] outside my head' (p. 36).

— What is the difference, according to Sethe, between a memory and a 'rememory'?

DISCUSS . . .

— If you are in a group, get together and discuss this distinction. Before you do this, you might like to break into smaller groups to discuss particular issues raised within the text:

● How does this version of memory alter our understanding of the past?

- In what ways does this give memory particular powers over the person remembering?
- We normally consider memories to be personal, but how does the idea that they exist 'outside my head' contradict this? If we accept this version, who owns memories?
- Is Sethe defining what it means to share a memory, or to have a 'collective' memory? How do you understand these terms?

— You might prefer to pick one topic and debate it in a larger group in relation to this section. Or you could take one of the questions raised and find textual evidence to discuss it throughout the novel as a whole.

— The theme of memory is important throughout the novel and one that you will be sure to return to. You might like to compare your ideas as you develop an understanding of the text, thinking about how they change as you read.

PART ONE
SECTION 5 (pp. 38–42)

Focus on: language and tone

DEVELOP . . .

— In this section Sethe moves from thinking about the past to focusing on her future with Paul D. In what ways is the text more positive at this point?

— Think particularly about the focus on 'colour' and colourful images here:

- How does this shift affect the mood and tone at this point?
- Does the discussion of colours lift or depress you as a reader?

- Think about the reasons for your answers.

REASSESS . . .

— Focus on the final line of the section. How does this affect the mood conjured by Sethe's discussion of colour?

Focus on: songs

RESEARCH . . .

— Songs were an important part of slave culture. Use the bibliography at the back of this book to aid you as you research the history of slave songs. You could either try and find out something about the songs quoted (p. 40) or you could attempt a more general search. Why are they such a valuable cultural resource? How are they used to express communal concerns? Why was it so difficult for slaves to record feelings, attitudes and experiences? How are songs used to pass on news and messages, as well as for emotional purposes? Refer to the exercise in the Contexts section on p. 83.

ACCUMULATE . . .

— If you are working in a group you might like to pick a particular topic or angle each and to pool your resources when you have conducted your research. How does your research into slave songs enhance your knowledge of the history and culture of slaves and the 'Institution of Slavery'?

PART ONE

Looking over Part One, sections 1–5

QUESTIONS FOR DISCUSSION OR ESSAYS
1.   Consider the treatment of either the theme of death or the theme of absence in the opening sections of *Beloved*.

2.   What kinds of literary genres are employed in Toni Morrison's novel so far?

3.   What is a 'rememory', and in how many different ways does it appear in these sections?

4.   Analyse the treatment of colour in the novel so far.

PART ONE
SECTION 6 (pp. 43–9)

Focus on: the theme of adolescence

ANALYSE . . .
— Paying particular attention to the relationship between Paul D and Denver, think about how Denver tests her relationship with her mother through her interaction with Paul D, firstly in her questioning of him (pp. 43–6) and then in their shared day out (pp. 46–9).

RELATE AND DISCUSS . . .
— Consider how Denver's relationship extends into our common experience. Think about a time when you challenged someone's authority over you – in what ways did your reactions differ from, or mirror Denver's? Here the suggested

outing provides a 'happy ending' to this section. Does this parallel your own experience?

— Discuss how you have reacted in a similar situation. Has it led to a confrontation between the person whose authority you respect and the one you are challenging? Is this a natural part of growing up? Was the resolution as swift and apparently amicable as is suggested in this section? Another way to ask this question is: how translatable is Denver's experience here?

PART ONE
SECTION 7 (pp. 50–6)

Focus on: the character of Beloved

ANALYSE . . .

— Examine closely the paragraphs that introduce Beloved (pp. 50–3, 55–6). Up until this point she has been discussed as a 'baby', but this section opens with the phrase 'A fully dressed woman' (p. 50). She is also unnamed. How does this confuse or complicate our attitude to the character?

— Pick out the phrases which you think characterise Beloved. For example:

- How does the link to her with 'women who drink champagne when there is nothing to celebrate' (p. 50) fit with your version of Beloved?
- What do you take Sethe's incontinence (p. 51) to signify?
- How do you interpret her need for sweet foods: 'It was as though sweet things were what she was born for' (p. 55)?

INTERPRET . . .

— Now reread the section, paying attention instead to the other characters' reactions to this new woman. Think about what their reactions tell you, both about Beloved and about the characters themselves. What strikes each of the characters first about Beloved?

RE-EVALUATE . . .

— When you have considered the relationship of the characters to Beloved, return to your analysis of her as she is presented. How is your version of her influenced by the other characters?

ANALYSE . . .

— Write a character analysis of Beloved at this point of introduction, incorporating within it how the other characters have informed your interpretation. Also, think about how expectation has influenced your interpretation.

BEAR IN MIND . . .

— What does Morrison achieve by withholding the protagonist named in the title until one-sixth of the way into the novel? How do your expectations influence her characterisation?

PART ONE
SECTION 8 (pp. 57–63)

Focus on: narrator versus narrated

EXAMINE . . .

— ' "Tell me," said Beloved, smiling a wide happy smile. "Tell me your diamonds." It became a way to feed her' (p. 58). Morrison suggests in this phrase the power of storytelling within the novel. Examine the theme of narration in this section of the story, thinking about control. We are used to thinking of the narrator as the controller of the narrative, but is this the case in this novel?

— Pay close attention to the questions Beloved asks throughout the story. Who is in control of this story: is it Beloved or Sethe?

REFRESH AND COMPARE . . .

— Think about the nature of narrators in this text and compare it to your consideration of 'memory'. Go back and look at your notes on pp. 28–38. You would expect the narrator to control the person, but this is complicated in the novel, as Beloved seems to be more in charge of the story than Sethe herself. How does this parallel Morrison's treatment of memory (see section 4)? How are narratives and memories connected in this section?

PONDER AND TALK THROUGH . . .

— Spend some time thinking and talking about the complex relationship of narratives and stories to memories in this novel. Use this section as a discussion example, thinking about how memories support people: try and give an instance of being comforted by a memory. Is this how the story works for Beloved and Denver?

— Do stories work in the same way for communities? Is that how narratives operate for the community within 124? Why does Denver feel excluded from the stories (p. 62)? Can you give examples of stories that your group finds sustaining? (You might like to think about 'urban myths', for example, or films or songs that you find cheer you up.)

PART ONE
SECTION 9 (pp. 64–73)

Focus on: the theme of knowledge

DETAIL AND CONTRAST . . .

— Using the character of Paul D, consider this section's discussion of 'knowledge'. Compare Paul D's questioning of Beloved (pp. 64–8) with his conversation with Sethe where he tells her what she didn't know about her husband's leaving her (pp. 68–73).

— Paul is at both ends of the spectrum here, as he both gives and requests information. Does he suggest that knowledge is a good thing? Is it useful? What does Morrison suggest by putting him in both roles?

— Now think about what you take 'knowledge' to mean. Is it a positive notion? What do you associate it with? Is this the same version of 'knowledge' that you are given by Paul D? Does he believe it to be useful and constructive?

— Or does knowledge seem slippery in this section? Does Paul D get productive answers to his questioning of Beloved?

EVALUATE . . .

— Look now at the final paragraphs of the section (pp. 72–3). How is Sethe's reaction a challenge to Paul D's desire for knowledge? How does it fit with the definition of knowledge that you have constructed through your own understanding, and through the character of Paul D?

PART ONE

Looking over Part One, sections 6–9

QUESTIONS FOR DISCUSSION OR ESSAYS

1. Why is this novel called *Beloved*?

2. 'Tell me your diamonds,' says Beloved on p. 58. How might this injunction relate to the novel as a whole?

3. Consider the effects created by the variety of narrative points of view offered in the novel so far.

4. Discuss the relationship of the past to the present as it is presented in the novel so far.

PART ONE
SECTION 10 (pp. 74–85)

Focus on: origins

READ CLOSELY . . .

— In this section Denver tells Beloved the story of her birth. Work your way through the passage, paying particular attention to the parts that are important to Denver. How does Denver describe her birth? Who are the people that feature in the story?

— Denver regards her origins as linked both to her mother and to Amy Denver. What are the differences in the roles these women play? How does she describe her relationship to them?

ANALYSE . . .

— When you have looked at the description Denver gives of

42

origins here, think about the impact this story has upon the character of Denver. Consider:

- Amy Denver – how does her whiteness influence Denver?
- Sethe – does the bond between her and Amy influence Sethe, and if so, how? What does this mean for Denver?
- Location – where is Denver born, and does she think of the place of her birth as an origin?

EXTEND . . .

— When you have thought about this passage and the questions raised, take your analysis of Denver's origins and think about how other characters talk about their own origins. You could focus on Sethe, Baby Suggs, Beloved or Paul D. How do their attitudes mirror/differ from Denver's. You may want to discuss the text as a whole, thinking about the theme of origins, or 'roots'. Are other characters interested in their 'roots' and where they came from? If so, in what ways?

PART ONE
SECTION 11 (pp. 86–94)

Focus on: 'the Clearing'

CONCEPTUALISE . . .

— Read the description of 'the Clearing' (p. 86) and try to conjure up an image of the space described. Think about how it looks physically: for example, imagine how dense the woodland surrounding it is. What time of year is it in your mental picture? How big is the space?

LIST AND ANALYSE . . .

— When you have thought about your image of the Clearing,

list the words Morrison uses to describe it. How does this influence your picture? What do the words suggest about the Clearing?

DEVELOP . . .

— Thinking about the list of words you have identified, develop your idea of what sort of space the Clearing is. What is the mood: is it calming? Scary? What kind of space is it: is it a meeting space, like a market? Is it a religious space? Is it a private or a communal place?

COMPARE AND DISCUSS . . .

— Get together in groups and compare your answers to these questions. How do you understand the Clearing? You might like to discuss the differences between the Clearing as a space and what you think it represents, and the house at 124.

Focus on: the 'Underground Railroad'

RESEARCH . . .

— Sethe journeys safely to 124 with the help of a number of people. The Underground Railroad (pp. 91–4) was a network of individuals devoted to helping slaves escape to freedom in the northern states. Using the bibliography and your own resources, research the Underground Railroad – you might like to try using it as a phrase in an Internet search. What can you discover about the role of this network in the emancipation of slaves? You could look at other novels that deal with slaves' journeys north, such as Harriet Beecher Stowe's novel *Uncle Tom's Cabin* (1852), or Frederick Douglass' *Narrative of the life of Frederick Douglass* (1845). How does *Beloved* tie in with this genre?

RELATE . . .

— How has your research developed your understanding of

the text? Has it altered your attitude to any or all of the characters? Think specifically about how your 'knowledge' of the Underground Railroad changes your understanding of this novel. Then, if you are also working on *Jazz* or *Paradise*, ask how your understanding of slave history influences other novels in the trilogy.

PART ONE
SECTION 12 (pp. 94–100)

Focus on: the theme of danger

CONSIDER . . .

— Examine the idea of danger. Do you consider the Clearing to be a dangerous or a safe place? Who do you think is being attacked, and who is the attacker? Who is being protected? As you analyse these questions you will come up with complicated responses; it is difficult to be sure about who gives Sethe the bruises, for she herself is not sure: 'Baby Suggs had not choked her as first she thought' (p. 98).

— Spend some time focusing on this ambivalence that the danger here is difficult to deduce. While focusing on this, consider the motives for the attack. Why would Baby Suggs or Beloved want to hurt or kill Sethe? What is the danger, or threat, here?

ASSOCIATE . . .

— When you have considered the danger or threat in this episode, think about what it means for the text as a whole: does it act as a warning? Are characters altered as we see them reacting to danger? How do your perceptions of Sethe, Beloved and Denver shift at this point?

— Come back to the question of 'danger' as you encounter

threatening and dangerous incidents in the progression of the novel. Is this the first overtly dangerous situation, or would you choose an earlier example of danger? Jot down the reasons for your choice.

PART ONE
SECTION 13 (pp. 100–5)

Focus on: the character of Denver

EXAMINE . . .

— In this section Denver is seen relating to a whole new community. While she is at school she is asked, 'Didn't your mother get locked away for murder? Wasn't you in there with her when she went?' (p. 104). Examine the events in this section and their consequences for Denver. How do they fundamentally change her? Does it alter your own attitude to the character?

— Also consider whether or not it is a device – a means of imparting information to the reader. If so, how does it affect the reader to learn things with Denver? Does it increase our sympathy for her? If so, why?

EXTEND . . .

— Examine both the character of Denver and the function of the character of Denver within the text. Take evidence from wherever you find it; do not restrict yourself to this specific section. Do we often learn things with her? Or is she one of the primary narrators? How is she different from the other main protagonists?

PART ONE
SECTION 14 (pp. 106–13)

Focus on: masculinity

DISCOVER . . .

— Here the text focuses on Paul D's escape from 'Sweet Home'. Frequently in debates about slavery men are described as emasculated. Use the glossary at the end of this book and dictionaries to explain what this means.

RELATE . . .

— When you are happy with your understanding of the term, go back to this passage. How is Paul D's powerlessness characterised by masculine and feminine characteristics? For example, think about the choice of 'her' in the following sentences: 'Life was dead. Paul D beat her butt all day every day till there was still not a whimper in her' (p. 109).

— How is Paul D emasculated by slavery? Pick out specific examples, such as the abuse of the guards (pp. 107–8). Follow through your analysis by looking at the difference in attitudes when the men work collectively to escape. How is their sense of maleness re-established here?

— Question the association of maleness with authority in this section. Think about its complexity in the passage as the guards taunt and assault the men compared with when they have broken free. Is there a straightforward link between masculinity and power?

RETURN . . .

— Come back to the discussion when you have finished your analysis of the novel and discuss this question in terms of Sethe's actions. Are they anti- or un-female? How is her gender used to explain or condemn her actions?

PART ONE

Looking over Part One, sections 10–14

QUESTIONS FOR DISCUSSION OR ESSAYS

1.   How significant is a knowledge of origin in creating a sense of identity in the novel so far?

2.   How does Morrison create and employ a sense of place in the novel?

3.   'How you see and what you see determines who and what you will be.' Discuss, in relation to the themes of *Beloved*.

4.   How important is it to have an understanding of the systems of slavery in constructing an appreciation of Morrison's *Beloved*?

5.   Consider the treatment of authority and the abuse of power so far in *Beloved*.

6.   From your reading so far, is Morrison optimistic about the possibilities of relationships between men and women, or not?

PART ONE
SECTION 15 (pp. 114–17)

Focus on: the theme of sex

ASSESS . . .
— Look at the encounter here between Beloved and Paul D. Which of the following words would you choose to characterise the incident:

- Lust?
- Love?
- Seduction?
- Rape?
- Accident?
- Abuse?

— When you have chosen a term, note beside it the reasons for your choice.

— Then think about who you consider to be in control of the situation. Does Paul D seduce Beloved? Or does she seduce him? Again, develop the argument that supports your choice.

REASSESS . . .

— In the light of your analysis, return to the two characters. How does this incident change your attitude to Paul D and to Beloved?

— If you undertook the exercise focusing on Paul D (section 14), look at the language used in the description of their sexual encounter. How is gender used here?

PART ONE
SECTION 16 (pp. 118–24)

Focus on: language and tone, the third-person narrator

DEFINE . . .

— The relationship between Beloved and Denver is narrated in the third person here. What does it mean to describe a piece of text as having a 'third-person' narrator?

EXAMINE . . .

— Read closely through the section, looking at whose position the narrator takes. Is the narrative viewpoint more closely linked to Beloved or Denver? With whom does the narrator appear to sympathise? Does the focus shift or remain constant? Has the narrative revealed Beloved's thoughts at any point so far? Think about how the style of narration influences your understanding.

EXPERIMENT AND TRANSFORM . . .

— Choose a paragraph that particularly interests you, and then rewrite it in the first person. (For example: 'Denver suggests warming up some cider, while her mind races to something she might do . . .' (p. 121) becomes '"I know, why don't I warm up some cider," I said, trying desperately to think of something I might do . . .')

— How does this alter your perspective on the dialogue? How much influence does the unnamed narrator have on the reader? How is their position characterised?

— Think about how this highlights the role of the narrator in the novel. You might like to pick another passage from somewhere else in the text and try the experiment again; or, if you are in a group, you might prefer each to take one passage and compare the differences in your rewrites.

DISCUSS . . .

— Get together and talk about how this experiment has highlighted the role of the narrator in this novel. What questions has it raised for you? Does it change your views of the characters? How often do they narrate their own stories?

PART ONE
SECTION 17 (pp. 125–32)

Focus on: Sethe

ANALYSE AND DISCUSS . . .
— 'You *need* some babies, somebody to play with in the snow' (p. 130). Sethe and Paul D have a positive conversation about the possibility of more children. Analyse Sethe in this passage and think about what defines her character. Imagine you are describing her to someone who has not read the book, and sketch out the terms and phrases that you think epitomise her.
— To what extent do you think Sethe is defined by her role as a mother? What impact does motherhood have on her relationship with Paul D?

RE-INTERPRET . . .
— Come back to this question throughout your analysis, and think about what it means to be a mother. How is motherhood defined through Sethe? Is she presented as a good mother?
— When you have formed an opinion about Sethe as 'mother', focus on the relationship of motherhood to slavery. How does slavery undermine ideas of motherhood? What examples in the text highlight the opposition between being a mother and being a slave?

PART ONE
SECTION 18 (pp. 133–4)

Focus on: style and structure

COUNT . . .
— Look at the page numbers – what point is this in the novel?

CONSIDER . . .
— What are you told in this section? Think about how your interpretation of it is influenced by where it is placed in the novel. How does such a short segment divide up the novel's structure?
— How does the structure, or shape, of the novel influence your interpretation? For example, what is highlighted here for Beloved? What significant change is signalled, and why does Morrison ensure it is at the centre of the book? What changes in the narrative point of view? What mood does it establish for the second half of the text?

PART ONE

Looking over Part One, sections 15–18

QUESTIONS FOR DISCUSSION OR ESSAYS
1. Analyse the ways in which the text promotes reactions of disgust, sympathy, horror and condemnation in the reader.

2. How is time treated in this novel, and to what effect?

3. Explain the narrative structure of the novel so far and discuss the effects created by it.

PART ONE
SECTION 19 (pp. 135–47)

Focus on: time

INFER . . .
This section opens with an abrupt time-shift. At the end of

the previous section Sethe and Paul D are together, and this one opens in the present tense, but with a character who is already dead: 'In the back of Baby Suggs' mind' (p. 135).

— Think about the effect of this time-shift upon the reader. Is it immediately clear what time the action is taking place in? How far back has the action shifted?

DISTINGUISH AND COMPARE . . .

— The reader is given the substance of the plot at this point in the novel. We are told about the events that motivate the novel. Pick out the particular events that take place in this section.

— You may want to construct a timeline for yourself of the series of events in chronological order in *Beloved*. Then compare this to the action of the novel itself. What are the differences between the plot and the timeline?

ANALYSE WITH CLOSE READING . . .

— The theme of time is hugely important in *Beloved*. Reread the section, focusing on the idea of time. How is time manipulated in the text? For example:

- What tense is this section written in?
- What difference does it make to the reader hearing about the events in the present tense?
- What is Baby Suggs referring to at the end of the section when she is 'feeling a dark and coming thing' (p. 147)?
- What events do we know at this point lie in the future for Baby Suggs?
- What is in the future in this section?

— Think about how the reader already knows the future at this point. How does this increase the dramatic tension of the novel? Consider how different the novel would be if this were the opening chapter, or if it followed your chronological time-line.

— How is the novel's handling of time used to create dramatic tension?

PART ONE
SECTION 20 (pp. 148–53)

Focus on: genre

DETERMINE . . .

— In what ways are the events in this section at the centre, or crux, of the novel? Pick out what they are, and think about why they are so central to the book.

CATEGORISE . . .

— Look at how the events at the centre of the novel are presented. What genres would you say best describe this section:

● Historical novel?
● Horror?
● Tragedy?
● Comedy?
● Myth?

EXPLORE . . .

— Set out what defines the genre, or genres, you have chosen. In what ways does the section conform to the genre of horror, for example? Is it through suspense? Blood and gore? Or is it a tragedy precisely because of the way in which the bloody actions are described?

— The action of the section is central to the novel. Do you think the genre you have identified for this section covers the novel as a whole? Explore the reasons for your choices. Would you want to choose another genre from the list or to pick an entirely new one for the whole novel?

— Think about why choosing a genre for this book is so complicated, and come back to your choice as you work your way through the text. Does it remain the same? What elements change your decision?

PART ONE
SECTION 21 (pp. 154–65)

Focus on: forms of writing – newspapers

RESEARCH . . .

— Look particularly at the beginning of this section, from 'He smoothed the clipping with his fingers and peered at it . . .' (p. 154 to p. 158).

— Paul D learns of Beloved's murder in a newspaper clipping that Stamp Paid gives to him. Morrison was inspired to write the novel when she came across a newspaper clipping about Margaret Garner. Using the bibliography in this book, and through your own research, find out who Margaret Garner was. What was her story?

INTERPRET . . .

— How do different forms of writing influence what we read? Are our expectations different when we pick up a newspaper from when we read a magazine or novel? If so, in what way?

— How does Morrison use the newspaper in this section? Does it have a different impact on Paul D from other forms of communication? If so, why?

— List the different kinds of writing and narration that you come across, from the number of narrators to newspapers and gravestones.

— Think about how Morrison employs different methods of communication to convey different ideas in the novel. You might like to pick two forms and compare their effects.

Focus on: the theme of intimacy

REVISE . . .

— Intimacy between Paul D and Sethe was highlighted in the discussion of Part One, section 3. Here the text returns to focusing on the couple's relationship. How has their relationship altered?

DETAIL . . .

— Look particularly closely at the language here. Trees, for example, were highlighted in the first discussion of intimacy, so work through this section looking for tree imagery (p. 165). How has the image changed, and what does this suggest?

RE-EVALUATE . . .

— How has the revelation to both Paul D and the reader altered our understanding of Sethe? How has closeness or intimacy been damaged by the direct knowledge of Beloved's death?

— The text highlights how complicated intimacy is here. Looking at this section, think about how the couple's closeness is disturbed. It may be useful to divide the topic into different kinds of intimacy, such as emotional and sexual intimacy.

INCORPORATE . . .

— Use the bibliography, the research you have done and the information in the introduction to provide a context for the breakdown in intimacy between Sethe and Paul D. This means that you need to think about Sethe and Paul as escaped slaves. How does your knowledge of slavery and its history help to explain Sethe's actions? In what ways does your consideration of the historical context alter your attitude?

BRING TOGETHER . . .
— Return to the question of intimacy. Either in discussion or in the form of an essay, think about how slavery destroys the intimacy between Paul and Sethe. This question could be rephrased as: was Sethe forced to kill Beloved? Or: did the 'Institution of Slavery' leave Sethe any choice?

PART ONE

Looking over Part One, sections 19–21

QUESTIONS FOR DISCUSSION OR ESSAYS
1.   'Murder is never justified.' Discuss with reference to Part One of *Beloved*.

2.   'The history of a race can only be told through the history of an individual.' Discuss.

3.   Consider notions of motherhood in Part One of *Beloved*.

PART TWO
SECTION I (pp. 169–83)

Focus on: language and tone

DESCRIBE AND INTERPRET . . .
— Looking particularly at the beginning of the section (pp. 169–73), identify the descriptions of the house, 124. When

an object is described as if it were a living individual, it is called *personification*. Look at the examples you have taken from this section: in what ways is the house personified?

— When you have looked at how 124 is personified here, think about where else in the novel the house is treated as if it were a person, and consider the effects of this personification.

Focus on: the character of Stamp Paid

SKETCH AND ASSESS . . .

— In this section the reader is guided through the events at 124 from the perspective of Stamp Paid. Working through this section, sketch out what we learn about Stamp as a character here. Pick a piece of textual evidence to support each claim you make about his character.

— Stamp discusses what it means to be a narrator (pp. 169–73, 176–81). Examine his discussion of the guilt of telling Paul D the story, and the account of his attempts to visit 124. How does filtering the action through Stamp change your attitude to what occurs at 124? What difference does it make, hearing the account of Beloved's death from an 'outsider'?

COMPARE . . .

— Stamp Paid is the second male narrator. Compare his first-hand account of the traumas that he witnesses with Paul D's reaction to Sethe when she tells him what happened (pp. 164–5). While conducting your comparison, think about the following issues:

● Why does Morrison choose to have Stamp Paid narrate a version of the events at 124?
● Why choose a male, and not a female, narrator?
● How would this story differ if Baby Suggs, Sethe or even Beloved narrated it?

Focus on: the theme of playing

ANALYSE . . .

— In between Stamp Paid's accounts of 124 the narrator tells us that 'While Stamp Paid was making up his mind to visit 124 for Baby Suggs' sake, Sethe was trying to take her advice' (p. 173). Look particularly at these sections (pp. 173–6, 181–3) and identify examples of the language of play used here.

— Think about descriptions of play. For example, you may expect a light and jolly tone, jokes, humorous incidents or a positive mood. Does this passage meet your expectations or does it surprise you? Highlight examples to support your argument.

INTERPRET . . .

— When you have examined the ice-skating narratives, think about the section as a whole. Use the following questions to interpret the issues that it raises:

● Why do you think Morrison chooses to give us an account of ice-skating here?
● What is the purpose for the reader of a happy afternoon's ice-skating? How does it alter the mood of this part of the text?
● How are the descriptions of the day ice-skating used to juxtapose Stamp Paid's sections?

PART TWO
SECTION 2 (pp. 183–8)

Focus on: the theme of community

EXAMINE AND COMPARE . . .

— In this section two journeys take place simultaneously: Sethe travels to work, and Stamp travels to see Ella. Look at the intertwined journeys. How is a sense of community created by narrating two separate stories alongside one another? What linguistically links the two characters? How does the plot itself link them?

— If you want to explore this issue, look at other texts that link characters by weaving separate stories together: *Dubliners* (1914), for example, by James Joyce, or *Hey Yeah Right Get a Life* (2000) by Helen Simpson.

EXPLORE . . .

— When you have looked at how the two narratives are linked, think about what you understand by the word 'community'. What are the links that you think tie the two characters together? What kinds of associations create a community here: guilt, family, religion, skin colour, slave versus slave owner?

— Then look at the conversation that takes place between Stamp and Ella. How is this dialogue used to reinforce a sense of community? Spend some time selecting the various ways in which community and the idea of links between individuals are established here.

PART TWO
SECTION 3 (pp. 188–99)

Focus on: the theme of ownership – being owned

DISTINGUISH . . .

— Sethe remembers her life at 'Sweet Home' in the bulk of this section (pp. 190–8). Look particularly at the characters of Mr and Mrs Garner and Schoolteacher. Here you are given two different 'owners'. Pick out the differences between Schoolteacher and the Garners. You might like to do this in note or table form.

— What does Sethe tell the reader about the different kinds of 'ownership' that she is subject to at Sweet Home? While you are considering this, bear in mind the following kinds of ownership:

- Physical: how do the two owners control Sethe and the men physically? What are they stopped from doing? How physically free are they?
- Emotional/psychological: in what ways are the slaves controlled mentally? Look for example at Sixo's argument with Schoolteacher (p. 190).
- Sexual: how is Sethe 'owned' as a sexual object? (To answer this you may want to refer to other parts of the novel, as well as this section.)

CONSIDER . . .

— When you have looked at the difference between the Garners and Schoolteacher, think about why Morrison gives the reader these examples of different types of ownership. Why do you think she shows us different kinds of cruelty?

— Once again, by placing the two experiences next to one another she is linking them. Why do you think she wants the reader to think about these different kinds of ownership?

BROADEN . . .

— Use this focused analysis for a broader discussion of 'ownership'. Work as a group to talk about the different kinds of ownership outlined above. Would you want to add another category? How does Morrison use the Garners to highlight that abuse is not simply a physical issue? Refer to the book as a whole.

PART TWO

Looking over Part Two, sections 1–3

QUESTIONS FOR DISCUSSION OR ESSAYS

1. Consider the treatment of the theme of loss in these sections.

2. Compare the themes of growth and atrophy in the novel so far.

PART TWO
SECTION 4 (pp. 200–4)

Focus on: the theme of motherhood

DETERMINE AND DEVELOP . . .

— This chapter is framed by Sethe saying that Beloved is her 'daughter' (pp. 200, 204). Work your way through this section treating it as a discussion of motherhood. Which particular words, phrases, metaphors and similes set this up as a mother–daughter conversation? Who is speaking, and to whom are they speaking?

— Select the sentences that suggest motherhood to you. How

are they used to explain Sethe's killing of Beloved? Is Sethe here defending her actions as motherly? If so, how?

EXTEND . . .

— Consider how your analysis of this section gives you an insight into the character of Sethe. Does it help to explain her behaviour? Does the reader feel closer to her at the end of the section, or is this a justification of murder that makes the reader suspicious?

— Take this set of ideas further by thinking about the relationship of motherhood to slavery. Sethe talks about her own mother (p. 200). What, according to Sethe, does slavery deny mothers?

— Is the only choice, when faced with sending her children back to be slaves, to kill them? How does her defence of her behaviour attack slavery? If you are interested in this topic, look at *Uncle Tom's Cabin*, which debates the consequences of slavery upon the relationship between the mother and child. (You might refer also to the exercise on p. 82.)

PART TWO
SECTION 5 (pp. 205–9)

Focus on: stories

COUNT AND CATEGORISE . . .

— How many stories are there in Denver's section? What kinds of stories does Denver repeat? Create suitable categories – such as myth, horror, children's stories, romance, history – and make notes as to what motivated your choices.

ASSESS . . .

— When you have grouped the stories, return to this section

and look at Denver's justification for them. How does she react to the stories she tells? For example, is she horrified by the stories you have classed as 'horror'? How does her reaction influence yours?

— Develop this analysis by focusing on the power of these stories. Why does Denver consider them to be important? For example, how do Baby Suggs's stories of Denver's father empower her?

— You might want to return to the earlier discussion of story-telling. How do the conclusions you reached in your analysis of narrators in Part One, section 8 fit with your reading of Denver's stories?

PART TWO
SECTION 6 (pp. 210–13)

Focus on: language and style

EXPERIMENT . . .

— The style of this section is unusual, in that it has no punctuation. Divide it into passages and then attempt to punctuate a paragraph. Use as many different kinds of punctuation as you can: brackets, speech marks, apostrophes, hyphens, as well as full stops and commas.

— How does your punctuation alter the meaning of the passage you have chosen? Which decisions did you find particularly difficult?

— Come together in a group and discuss how the exercise made you think really carefully about what is being said. Is it always easy to know who is speaking, or who is being spoken to? Do identities merge when you are not sure where one sentence ends and another begins?

ASSESS . . .

— Why do you think Morrison deliberately left this section unpunctuated?

— How does Beloved's merging with other characters' voices in this section represent her relationship with Sethe and Denver in the text? (You might want to look beyond this section as you think about these questions.)

COMPARE . . .

— Read the final section of James Joyce's *Ulysses* (1922). Though there is some editorial dispute about Joyce's intentions in the presentation of the book overall, there is no doubt that this famous section was meant to appear very lightly and idiosyncratically punctuated. Compare Joyce's method with Morrison's. In what ways are the aims of the two writers similar as they convey the private thoughts of their characters?

PART TWO
SECTION 7 (pp. 214–17)

Focus on: style and tone, and poetic method

ARGUE AND DEVELOP . . .

— Look at the second part of this section (pp. 215–17). Could this passage be described as a poem? In order to consider the question fully, think about what makes a poem. What features do you expect it to have, in terms of structure and language? Does this section meet your expectations? Select phrases, metaphors and similes that you consider to be poetic.

— How does your consideration of this section as a poem change your attitude to it? Who is speaking? How many narrative voices are there? To what extent do they blend into one?

STEP BACK AND INTERROGATE . . .

— Extend your analysis to take in the whole text. You may even want to go as far as thinking about all three texts – how many different forms of communication, or styles of writing, are there? Do you find examples of poems anywhere else?

— Focus on what different types of writing suggest. Think about how some forms of writing are thought to be more intellectual than others. Come back to this as you work your way through the text.

PART TWO

Looking over Part Two, sections 4–7

Focus on: the number three

RECONSIDER . . .

— Think about Part Two as a whole: how many sections make up Part Two? How many narrators are there, and who are they? How does this structure mirror the novel as a whole?

LIST . . .

The number three is highly significant in Western culture, as well as being a theme in this text. (You may want to turn to the overall consideration of the trilogy at the front of this book, which discusses various interpretations of the number three.)

— Jot down the various ways in which the text as a whole uses the number three.

EVALUATE . . .

— When you have examined occurrences of the number three in these sections and in the novel as a whole, you need to eval-

uate what you think the significance is in this central section
– why do you think Morrison places this trinity centrally?

— These are open-ended questions, and you need to consider
why three is culturally significant. Use Part Two of the novel
as the focus of your discussion of the number three. Draw on
the cultural significance highlighted in the introduction to the
trilogy earlier in this book. This is a major theme and one that
you will return to again and again in your analysis both of this
text and of the trilogy, so keep updating your thoughts as you
work through your criticism of *Beloved*.

Focus on: language and narrative links

COMPARE AND CONTRAST . . .

— Look at the opening sentences of sections 4–7. Looking
only at these sentences, think about how they provide a
narrative link between these sections. In what ways are they
similar? In what ways different? How do you think this tech-
nique affects the reader?

— Now look at the sections as they are treated individually,
but try and keep in mind the issues you have looked at in your
consideration of the group as a whole. Remember the links
between sections you have identified and the topics you have
highlighted.

QUESTIONS FOR DISCUSSION OR ESSAYS

1. Consider how the themes of the novel are reflected in the
linguistic and narrative methods adopted by Morrison.

2. Analyse the significance of the number three in these sections, and in the novel as a whole.

3. How important are names and naming in *Beloved*?

PART TWO
SECTION 8 (pp. 218–29)

Focus on: the theme of escape

RESEARCH AND DISCOVER . . .

— At this point the narrative flashes back to an attempted escape at 'Sweet Home'. Using the resources provided in this book find an account of an attempted escape from the southern states to the free northern states written at this period of American history. If you choose a long account, you may want to focus on only one part of it. Try and keep to the idea of an attempted escape.

— If you undertook research into the Underground Railroad, you might now want to extend that work to find a particular account. Or you may prefer to approach this topic from a fresh angle.

COMPARE . . .

— How do the accounts you have discovered compare with this narrative of attempted escape? Paul talks about his confinement in animal terms: he observes a rooster, freer than him, 'smiling' at him (p. 229). Is similar imagery used in the account you have found?

— Turn your attention back to this section. How is the idea of escape important for the plot? Think about how many characters attempt to escape from situations.

— Examine what escape means in this novel. Is it a mainly physical form of escape that concerns the characters? If not, what other events could be described as 'escapes'? Would it be possible to describe Suggs's, or even Beloved's, death as an 'escape'?

PART TWO
SECTION 9 (pp. 230–5)

Focus on: mystery

ANALYSE . . .

— The end of the section is Stamp's question: 'Why? Why? Why? Why? Why?' (p. 235). This ends Part Two as well as the section. Think about these questions: they are indirect, and their repetition suggests a great mystery.

— Scan this section and pick out the various mysteries referred to here. For example, more than one explanation is offered for Beloved's appearance. How do these different suggestions create a sense of mystery?

EXPLORE . . .

— Think about this section as the end of Part Two. Focus on the idea of endings and conclusions. Are you provided with answers? Or are questions made more complicated? How does Stamp's and Paul's conversation create an air of suspense by prolonging mysteries?

PART TWO

Looking over Part Two, sections 8–9

QUESTIONS FOR DISCUSSION OR ESSAYS

1. List the narrative flash-backs used in these sections of the novel, and explain how they work and what effect they have on the telling of the story and on your reactions.

2. How are mystery and surprise built up in this part of the text?

3. Consider the metaphorical significance of the theme of escape in these sections, and in the novel as a whole.

PART THREE
SECTION I (pp. 239–44)

Focus on: the theme of natural versus unnatural

EXAMINE . . .

— This is the opening section of Part Three, and in this section Beloved begins to really take over 124. As Denver says, 'The mood changed, and the arguments began' (p. 241). First, look at the changes that occur in this section. What are the alterations that Denver notices? Does she think that it is only Beloved who is changing? What differences does she note in Sethe?

— Second, think about these changes in terms of natural versus unnatural. Pick out some of the examples of change that you have identified and look at how Denver characterises some behaviour as natural, or normal, and how she points out the unnatural changes in the other women at 124.

EXTEND . . .

— Once you have identified the ways in which Denver characterises some actions and attitudes as abnormal or unnatural, turn your focus solely on Beloved. To what extent is she an unnatural figure in this section? You might also like to think about the supernatural here:

- Note the words that you associate with the supernatural, and then think about how well they characterise Beloved.
- What is the difference between unnatural and supernatural behaviour?

— Use this discussion, and the work you have done on 'natural versus unnatural', and extend your enquiry to other sections of the novel. This may involve bringing in other examples of Beloved's 'unnaturalness', or you could turn the focus on another character, such as Sethe, and examine to what extent you consider her behaviour to be 'natural'.

PART THREE
SECTION 2 (pp. 245–62)

Focus on: the theme of community

CONSIDER . . .
— Community is a major theme in the novel; it is broken down here into sections, but bring your analysis together and think about the whole of section 2.

REFRESH . . .
— Part Two, section 2 also considered the idea of community, so turn back to your notes on this section. (If you have not yet attempted it, you might want to turn to it at this point.) Remind yourself of your thoughts about community. Now turn your attention to this passage, which concludes with the paragraph ending 'Why not the third generation as well?' (p. 252).

EVALUATE AND ASSESS . . .
— How are gestures and phrases used to suggest being part of the community outside 124 (pp. 245–9)? Look closely at Denver's conversation with Lady Jones: how is the community beyond 124 established here?
— When you have considered Denver's relationship with people outside 124, turn your attention to the second part of

the section (pp. 249–52), 'As Denver's outside life improved, her home life deteriorated' (p. 249). Assess the very different community within 124. How is the cooperation that Denver manages 'outside' contrasted with the life at 124?

DISCUSS . . .
— Discuss the differences between the two communities. Are they simply the opposite of one another, or do they share values? What is it that is working well for Denver, but proving disastrous for life within 124?

COMPARE . . .
— Denver's decision to step back into the community is the focus of this segment. Look at her description of her journey through the town. How does she physically re-enter the community here? Pay particular attention to the details of the journey.
— Using your earlier analysis, compare Denver's journey with the journeys you looked at in Part Two, section 2. Think about what the differences suggest about being part of a community: is Denver included, where the others have been excluded, or do the sections mirror each other?

LIST . . .
— In the next part of the section (p. 252–62) we see the community coming together to help the family at 124. Pick out the individuals who make up this community. Who are the leaders of the attempt to drive Beloved from 124? Look over your list and use it to establish what links bind the community. Is it formed predominantly along gender lines? What role does race play in its formation? Is it a solely black or white community?

DETAIL . . .
— Work closely with the text to establish who forms this com-

munity and what values its members share.
— Look for references to other communities, such as the
people who gathered at 'the Clearing'. What values does the
Clearing represent here. What do the people who travel to 124
have as their common aim?

BRING TOGETHER . . .
— Now think about this large section as a whole. Use some
or all of the questions below to stimulate your ideas. These
take you into the novel as a whole, and ask you to think about
wider considerations, both for the text and for you as a reader:

● What conclusions have you formed about the communi-
  ties represented here?
● How important is community to the novel?
● Has your attitude to what it means to belong to a com-
  munity changed as you have analysed the novel?
● What communities do you belong to? What defines them?
● What are the values that you share with the other individ-
  uals in that community?

PART THREE
SECTION 3 (pp. 263–73)

Focus on: Paul D

CHARACTERISE . . .
— Paul D returns to 124 at the end of the novel. How does
his character react in this final section? What changes do you
notice in his attitudes to Sethe, Denver and Beloved? Look at
imagery, metaphor and simile, and pick out specific phrases
that support your character analysis.

AMALGAMATE . . .

— Bring together your previous discussions of Paul D and combine them with this final analysis. Looking at your work as a whole, what developments do you notice in the character? How have his relationships with other characters altered? Is he now a member of the family at 124?

BROADEN . . .

— Extend your analysis and consider how Paul D's relationship with Beloved and her death change the reader's attitude to slavery. What does the reader learn about slavery through Paul D?

Focus on: genre

CONSIDER . . .

— Does Paul D's return to 124 make this a happy ending? Think about this question and then ponder its consequence for the genre of the novel. How does a consideration of whether or not this is a positive ending affect your attitude to the text?

FORM . . .

— If you are working in a group, come together and choose some genres for discussion – for example, fairy tale, horror, biography, history – that are evident in *Beloved* but make sure you do not simply use these examples; determine your own selection.

— When you have done this, talk through the reasons for your choices, paying particular attention to endings. How important are endings? How much do they influence you in your choice of genre?

— Bear in mind the relationship of the end to the beginning of the novel: are they similar? What qualities do they share?

Bring the final page of text into your discussion. How does it influence your decisions?

PART THREE
SECTION 4 (pp. 274–5)

Focus on: 'This is not a story to pass on'

INTERPRET . . .

— Focus on the phrase 'This is not a story to pass on' (p. 274). How many different meanings of this can you think of? Initially work individually, then come together as a group. Compare the different readings you have for the sentence.

— Why do you think this phrase is so highlighted at the conclusion of the novel? How many times is it used?

ANALYSE WITH CLOSE READING . . .

— Split this final section up and work on a paragraph each. Work together to establish what you believe to be the main point of your paragraph.

— How does the sentence 'This is not a story to pass on' affect your understanding of the passage you have chosen?

RE-INTERPRET . . .

— In the previous section the focus was on genre and how endings influence our understanding of novels. How does your analysis of the novel's closing paragraphs change, or perhaps reinforce, your reading of the novel as a whole?

CONCLUDE . . .

— Use the end of the novel to address questions about the text as a whole. (Use the overall discussion at the outset to remind yourself of major themes in the novel.) How do you understand the final word — is it a reference to a character, or an instruction? Is it positive or negative?

— Take your analysis full circle and return to an earlier question you were asked to consider in relation to this book: why is this novel called *Beloved*?

PART THREE

Looking over Part Three, sections 1–4

QUESTIONS FOR DISCUSSION OR ESSAYS

1. Discriminate between and discuss the relevance of, the terms 'natural', 'unnatural' and 'supernatural' in Part Three.

2. Consider the imagery of journeys and journeying in these sections.

Looking back over the whole novel

QUESTIONS FOR DISCUSSION OR ESSAYS

1. How can Morrison's *Beloved* be categorised in terms of genre?

2. Discuss the effect of the ending of *Beloved*.

3. Consider the metaphors and imagery to do with ghosts and haunting in the novel as a whole.

4. Analyse the narrative methods used by Morrison in *Beloved*.

5. 'We who are free, are we free?' Discuss, in relation to *Beloved*.

6. Morrison has been described as a writer who uses poetry

in prose. Show why this is an apt account of her language and style.

7. Discuss the significance of the past and of memory in *Beloved*.

8. Examine the ways in which narrative points of view are presented in *Beloved*, and the effects created by these.

9. Consider the way in which *Beloved* presents the theme of storytelling.

10. Read p. 14 of Morrison's interview and discuss whether you find Morrison's prose rich and ornate, or lean and understated.

11. Discuss notions of ownership in *Beloved*.

Contexts, comparisons and complementary readings

BELOVED

Context is important for the three novels in this trilogy, but it is, perhaps, of paramount concern in relation to *Beloved*. Many of the contextual suggestions made here expand on contexts touched upon within the detailed reading guides. The importance of slave narratives and history to this text make that overlap inevitable, although it is also productive. If you have looked at the more contextual exercises already suggested, then use them as a springboard for this fuller discussion. If you didn't look at those facets of the novel, then this section provides an opportunity to fully explore contextual and comparative analytic tools.

These sections suggest contextual and comparative ways of reading these three novels by Morrison. You can put your reading in a social, historical or literary context. You can make comparisons – again, social, literary or historical – with other texts or art works. Or you can choose complementary works (of whatever kind) – that is, art works, literary works, social reportage or facts that illuminate the text, by giving a framework to references that you currently find oblique. Some of the suggested contexts are directly connected to the books, in that they give you precise literary or social frames within which to situate the novel. In turn, these are either related to the period within which the novel is set, or to the time – now – when you are reading it. Some of these examples are designed to suggest books or other texts that may make useful sources for comparison (or for complementary purposes) when you are reading *Beloved*. Again, they may be related to literary or critical themes, or they may be relevant to social and cultural themes current 'then' or 'now'.

Also bear in mind the nature of a trilogy. Your contextual research for one of the texts will prove extremely useful in your work on the others. Equally, by reference to the themes that run throughout the trilogy, be aware that your analysis of individual texts could be used to inform another text. For example, here your research encourages a consideration of 'mothering', which reappears with a slightly different focus in both *Jazz* and *Paradise*. You might want to bring these discussions together to give you an overall response to the trilogy.

Focus on: the history of slavery

RESEARCH . . .

— *Beloved* is predicated upon the history of slavery. Look back over the interview with Morrison, paying attention to her discussion of the novel as 'alternate history' (pp. 11–12). Now, using the bibliographical resources provided here, as well as the Internet and libraries to which you have access, create a working knowledge of the historical context of the novel. Below is a list of key terms. Use them as a way of kick-starting your investigation by discovering what they mean:

- Chattel
- Octoroon
- Quadroon
- Mulatto
- Negro
- Emancipation
- Abolitionist.

— When you are clear about these specific terms, extend your research. Think about what it means to demarcate identities along colour-lines. Through your research you will also have come across some discussion of what it meant for slaves to be mulatto as opposed to octoroon – this will be developed later in the contextualisation, but bear in mind the value judgements being instituted here.

— Next, look into the following phrases, the historical keynotes that mark our understanding of the slave trade:

- The 'Institution of Slavery'
- The One-Drop Rule
- The Underground Railroad
- 'Passing'.

— What specific terms, events and practices do they refer to? Find out when the Fugitive Slave Act was passed in the United States – what powers did it give to slave owners? Also discover what the Emancipation Proclamation is – why was it so contentious?

COMPARE . . .

— Contrast the slave history you have researched with the text itself and with other seminal accounts of slavery. Harriet Beecher Stowe's novel, *Uncle Tom's Cabin* (1852), inspired President Abraham Lincoln to support emancipation and helped lead to the American Civil War. Look at her treatment of slaves on the basis of colour; for example, compare Eliza and George, who are able to 'pass', with the naughty Topsy.

— *Uncle Tom's Cabin* is important in slave narrative terms, but is complicated by Stowe's indirect knowledge of the 'Institution'. Look at the narratives of escaped slaves, such as Frederick Douglass's account of slave life in his *Narrative of the Life of Frederick Douglass, An American Slave.* (1845) or Harriet Jacob's story of slavery and her escape, *Incidents in the life of a slave girl* (1861). How do these accounts temper your response to *Beloved?*

CONTRAST AND INTERROGATE . . .

— Think about how much this contextualisation has informed your knowledge of slavery. How much did you know about slavery as an institution before you began this research? Look at Morrison's opening quotation:

> *Sixty Million*
> *and more.*

— Contrast this statement with your knowledge before you began your research. Think about this discrepancy, and ask yourself why the fate of such a historical massacre has remained outside your frame of historical reference, if it has. You might like to contrast it with your knowledge of 'the Holocaust'. Why is one historical event so well known to you in comparison with the other?

— Consider the politics of historical knowledge: who decides the histories we need to be aware of and those we are less acquainted with?

— Query particularly the relationship of the idea of the slave as an object for sale and the idea that the destruction of objects is somehow less culturally and historically traumatic than the killing of people.

Focus on: mothers

RESEARCH AND EXAMINE . . .

— One of the major weapons Harriet Beecher Stowe used in *Uncle Tom's Cabin* was the Cult of the Domestic. She sanctified motherhood as a counter to the practice of dividing up families in order to sell the children into slavery. Look particularly at three chapters of this novel. The first narrates Eliza's jumping across the Ohio River in order to save herself and her child from the hunters pursuing them. The second recounts the debate about the cruelty of separating families, as a mother (here a Senator's wife) responds to another mother's (albeit a slave's) grief. (The chapters are entitled 'The Mother's Struggle', 'Eliza's Escape' and 'In Which it Appears That a Senator is but a Man'.)

— Consider these excerpts in contrast to Sethe's murder of Beloved. How do these narratives challenge one another, in terms of their espousal of the values of motherhood?

— Think about Morrison's position in relation to this iconic text. How is she employing an infamous narrative here in contrast to Sethe's actions?

RELATE . . .

— Discuss this complex relationship; talk over your own concept of motherhood. What associations do you make with the term? Look at the suggestions below, and work in your own:

● Motherhood = kindliness, selflessness, unconditional love, goodness.

— Now re-introduce the historical context you have established through your research. How does the institution of slavery deny the slave the agency of the mother? How does this denial subvert the working definition of motherhood that you have constructed?

Focus on: storytelling

RESEARCH, PARALLEL, CONSIDER . . .

— The concept of storytelling is of great importance to this novel. Think, for example, of the paramount significance for Sethe of the gravestone.

— Gravestones are also of importance in the work of an author with whom Morrison is frequently compared, William Faulkner. You might like to compare the strategies of storytelling in *Beloved* with those in *Absalom, Absalom!* (1936).

— Compare the writers' employment of religious narratives: *Beloved* opens with a quote from the Bible and Faulkner's biblical references start with the novel's title. Use your comparison with *Absalom, Absalom!* to construct an analysis of the different storytelling modes that Morrison employs.

EXTEND . . .

— When you have identified the complexity of narrative genres to which Morrison refers (remember to look at her interview), think particularly about the history of oral narratives in the slave community. Discover, for example, by reading Frederick Douglass's *Narrative of the Life of Frederick Douglass*, how songs function here. Or, by using the anthologies and essay collections suggested in the bibliography (such as *The Harvard Guide to African American History*) discover the significance of oral narratives, both in terms of African heritage and as a way of undermining the literate slave owners.

— Use your research into oral narratives to inform your responses to the different narrative styles employed in *Beloved*. How does Morrison undermine the emphasis of literacy over orality?

Focus on: storytelling, colour prejudice and 'passing'

RESEARCH AND COMPARE . . .

— 'This is not a story to pass on.' There is at least one pun in Morrison's title. What does 'to pass' mean? As opposed to 'to pass on'? Read Nella Larsen's novel *Passing* (1929) and consider how the themes of that book relate to the themes of Morrison's novel. You could also read Judith Butler's critical account of the Larsen novel in *Bodies That Matter: On the Discursive Limits of Sex* (Routledge, 1993).

— What different kinds of 'passing' are there? Think about race, gender and sexuality in particular.

Examine these statements and assess your reactions to them:

- I'm glad to see this one's got a bit of black in her.
- You don't look like a lesbian.
- I used to be a feminist, but then I discovered men.
- 'I don't know about you old queens, but this old Queen needs a gin and tonic' (attributed to the Queen Mother).
- How many Irishmen does it take to change a light bulb? One to hold the bulb and three hundred thousand to turn the world.
- How many hippies does it take to change a light bulb? One to change the bulb and ten to share the experience.

Why are some stereotypes funny, but others not?

VINTAGE
LIVING
TEXTS

Jazz
IN CLOSE-UP

Reading guides for

JAZZ

BEFORE YOU BEGIN TO READ . . .
— Read the interview with Morrison. You will see there that she identifies a number of themes:

- Narrative voice
- Music, and particularly jazz
- Roots
- Identity
- Beauty and Horror.

Another theme that it may be useful to consider while reading the novel is:

- The City.

Reading activities: detailed analysis

SECTION 1 (pp. 1–5)

Focus on: openings

ANALYSE . . .

— 'Sth, I know that woman. She used to live with a flock of birds on Lenox Avenue' (p. 3). Stop and examine the opening sentence of this novel. Think about the expectations it sets up for the reader and list them. For example, who is speaking? Where is 'Lenox Avenue'?

— When you have drawn up a comprehensive list, turn to the rest of this opening section. How many of your questions are answered here? Is the reader told who is speaking? Does this opening section of the novel tell us in which city Lenox Avenue is?

COMPARE . . .

— Look over your questions and the evidence you have gleaned from the text. Which questions still remain unanswered? How comprehensive are the answers you have managed to establish? Compare the questions that do not have answers with those for which you have found textual evidence: are there any themes that link the unanswered questions together?

DISCUSS . . .

— Using the questions, answers and comparisons you have worked on, think about how this opening sentence establishes the themes of the novel. When you have provided answers working alone, compare the questions and answers you have devised with your group. Have you identified the same themes through your close reading?

— Think about the questions your analysis has provided. Are these 'mysteries'? How does the information that Morrison refuses to give you make the text magical or 'mysterious'? Or do the unanswered questions help to create the reader's expectations? Do we read the novel looking for particular information, or clues?

— As you work your way through the novel, keep an eye on your questions: are they ever answered? If so, at what point in the text are you given this textual evidence? What difference does it make to the novel *when* information is given, or how long it has been withheld? Are there any questions that remain unanswered? In what ways do they influence your interpretation of the novel?

SECTION 2 (pp. 5–9)

Focus on: plot

DETAIL . . .

— In this section the reader is given a great deal of information about the events of the novel. Work your way through and select that information. What are you told here about the plot of *Jazz?* Form a chronology, or timeline, of the events narrated here. You may find it a useful tool for analysis as you work your way through the novel.

CONSIDER . . .

— When you have created your timeline for the text, look at the amount of information you are given here. Are you surprised to find that you are told so much about the plot of the novel in the opening few pages? How does this change your attitude to the novel? Think particularly about the exercise you have just undertaken where you focused on the opening sentence: does the plot detail make the story less mysterious? If so, why? You may think that the effect upon the reader is to make the novel more mysterious, because your curiosity is aroused and you want to find out more details, or your interest may be in understanding *why* the characters behave as they do.

REFLECT AND ANALYSE . . .

— Before moving on to work on the bulk of the novel, think about the nature of the plot. What expectations, in terms of plot, has this opening section created for you as a reader? Think about how these plot details have affected your reading. For example, do you regard the novel as a murder mystery at this point? Throughout your analysis of the text the question of the plot in *Jazz* will come up again and again. You might like to devote a particular section of your notes to how the plot is constructed.

— Sketch out some issues affecting plot: for example, how many times are you told the same story? What changes occur in the plot? Which details are different in each telling? You will find these useful in focusing your attention, but also as a means of recording your changing attitudes to the novel. You will be able to examine how your developing analysis differs from the work you did at its opening.

Focus on: the theme of the City

MAP . . .

— 'I'm crazy about this City' (p. 7). Focus your attention particularly on the end of this section (pp. 7–9). Work your way through these pages, picking out the details of 'the City' that you are given here:

- Which specific places are referred to?
- Is the City itself identified?
- How does the speaker suggest the mood in the City they love?

— Use the information you are given here to establish the novel's context.

RESEARCH . . .

— Use the textual evidence from this section, the contexts, interview and bibliography to research this novel's setting. What makes Harlem in the 1920s so famous? What is the 'Harlem Renaissance', and who were the artists, musicians and writers who are identified with it?

— How does the 'Harlem Renaissance' form a backdrop to the novel? You might like to spend some time thinking about its relationship to the novel's title. How does *Jazz* provide a link?

SECTION 3 (pp. 9–17)

[This section finishes with the paragraph ending: 'Who never hurried anything but love' (p. 17).]

Focus on: the theme of death and remembrance

LIST . . .

— This section opens with the phrase 'Armistice was seven years old' (p. 9), referring to the end of the First World War. The idea of remembering deaths is important to the novel. Work your way through this section, paying particular attention to different memories of death. List the characters here who remember the dead and gone. Focus on Dorcas and the different ways in which she is remembered.

ESTABLISH . . .

— When you have detailed the different forms of remembrance, think about what it means to remember somebody. What events and forms of behaviour do you identify when you think about remembering the dead?

— You could use the 'armistice' as a model for formal acts of remembrance. Consider the ways in which we remember the First World War, and then extend this into other ways in which communities recognise the dead. Then think about less public types of remembrance. How do families in Western culture remember their dead?

EXAMINE AND INTERPRET . . .

— Look at the different forms of recognition that you have come up with, then turn your attention back to the novel. Do the characters also follow the formalities of remembrance? In what ways are the patterns that we recognise for honouring the dead broken here? Who breaks them?

— When you are considering this issue, bear in mind that some of the rules are broken in more subtle ways than others. For example, Violet's actions at the funeral are clearly not normal in terms of remembrance. However, also look at how Violet and Joe treat Dorcas's picture. Photographs of the dead are often an important part of preserving their memory. Think carefully about how this is distorted here.

EXTEND . . .

— When you have thought about how the text manipulates death and remembrance, you could either consider the topic in relation to the novel as a whole (returning to it when you have worked your way through *Jazz*), or you could take this thematic discussion further and look at either *Beloved* or *Paradise* in terms of this theme. How does remembrance form a central concern in either, or both, novels?

— Would you argue that death and remembrance form the thematic centre, or core, of the trilogy?

SECTION 4 (pp. 17–24)

Focus on: the idea of intention

EVALUATE . . .

Here the narrator tells the story of Violet's attempted abduction of a baby. 'When the baby was in her arms . . . Comfort settled itself in her stomach and a kind of skipping, running light traveled in her veins' (p. 19).

— Treat this story in isolation. Do you consider Violet to be actively trying to steal the child? What is it about the language of the incident that leads you to support or reject the notion that she is taking the baby? Work closely with the excerpt, establishing the specific phrases and clauses which have led you to the conclusion you have reached.

DISTINGUISH . . .

— When you have formed an initial response to this issue, return to this segment of text and look at who is telling you about the incident. How many perspectives do you get? Does

Violet, a witness, or an unnamed narrator, tell you of the events?

— Pick out which details of the story are given by which speaker? Who, in fact, narrates the substance of the story?

RE-EVALUATE . . .

— When you have looked at the different narrators, re-examine your analysis of the story. Has your attitude altered when you consider who is speaking? How much control over the story does Violet actually have? Do we, as readers, become more sympathetic to Violet if we regard her as not being in control of a story about her?

MOVE ON . . .

— You have worked on the idea of intention here – both the intention of the characters and of the narrators. Take this set of concerns on, to think about the narrative voice in this section . . .

Focus on: narrative voice

ASSESS . . .

'In *Jazz* the dynamite fuse to be lit was under the narrative voice' (p. 9). Morrison is speaking here about the novel in her collection of essays entitled *The House that Race Built*, where she talks about her deliberate intention to make the reader less secure about the authority of the speaker. She makes us wonder whether or not the teller's version of the story can be trusted.

You have distinguished the various narrative voices used, and thought about the ways in which the speaker who has told you of events has influenced your understanding of the character and of the story itself.

— Use the work you have already done on narrative voice and

extend your discussion to think about the reliability of the narrators in more detail.

— 'Her private cracks, however, were known to him. I call them cracks because that is what they are' (p. 22). Look particularly at the end of the section (pp. 22–4): what does the narrator mean by 'cracks' here? What is being suggested about Violet's mental state? How does this ensure that the reader regards Violet as an unreliable source of information? Does this version of Violet's understanding make us more likely to believe she did attempt to abduct the baby? If this is the case, why does the suggestion of 'cracks' in her consciousness call her skills as a reliable narrator into question?

EXPLORE . . .

— When you have considered Violet, turn your attention to the primary narrator. Focus on the following questions (keeping Morrison's quotation at the back of the mind as you do so):

● What does the reader know about who is speaking here?
● Do they witness the incident with the baby?
● What is their relationship to Violet and Joe?

REMEMBER . . .

— The idea of the unreliable narrator is, as Morrison herself suggests, a central concern of the novel. Attention will be refocused on the narrative voice as you work through the novel, but as you conduct your analysis, whenever you consider your reading to relate to this discussion, jot down your ideas. You will want to conduct an overview of the narrative voice and its unreliability when you have looked at the novel as a whole, and the notes you take will enable you to make a more comprehensive study of the text.

Focus on: Joe

CHARACTERISE . . .

— This section opens with an account of Joe and how separate the couple have now become: 'There is nothing for Violet . . . But for Joe it is different' (p. 28). Use this segment to form a profile of Joe.

— In order to characterise Joe, look at the two relationships that are explained here. The reader is given an account of Joe's current and past intimacies with both Dorcas and Violet.

— What differences do you note in his encounters with Dorcas as opposed to Violet? What phrases best describe the different relationships? When you have examined Joe in these different contexts, combine your results to produce a characterisation of Joe. How do the contradictions between his treatment of the women complicate his character?

— Write your character analysis up in essay format so that it reads in full sentences as opposed to note form. What phrases and descriptions have you used to support your analysis? Make sure your version of Joe is closely tied to this section of text, providing a justification for your interpretation of his character.

Focus on: the history of 'migration'

DISCOVER . . .

— Look at Joe's account of the couple's move to New York (pp. 29–37). You are given more than a personal history here, as it is not solely Joe and Violet who move. What historical narrative are you given through the account of Joe and Violet's journey to New York?

— Focus particularly on the different attitudes to the City that you are presented with here: what historical details are you given in this section? For example, the reader is told: 'The wave of black people running from want and violence crested in the 1870s' (p. 33), and that Joe and Violet are part of this movement. — Do some research to discover what historical events Morrison is referring to here. If you are in a group work together to discover what it means to 'migrate'.

COMBINE . . .

— If you are working in a group bring together the historical information you have discovered about the period to which the text refers here. Amalgamate your research to construct an answer to the following question (you may like to write up your answers as an essay or to keep to discussion notes): how does Morrison create an historical context for Joe and Violet in this section of the novel?

SECTION 6 (pp. 40–51)

Focus on: the theme of betrayal/being betrayed

INTERROGATE . . .

— 'Malvonne lived alone with newspapers and other people's stories printed in small books' (p. 40). The character Malvonne is introduced to the reader here. Think initially about how she functions as a character within the novel. You might like to consider her role in relation to the following questions:

● What purpose does she serve?
● How does her existence affect the plot?
● Why does Morrison introduce Malvonne into the story at this point?

EXTEND AND LINK . . .

— Keeping your critical attention centred on Malvonne, extend your analysis of her to ponder the theme of betrayal.

Scrutinise the language that characterises her: is she an active or passive character? How is she described in her relationship to the community – is she an active member of society? To her son, is she a controlling mother?

— Bring together your analysis of Malvonne, and your assessment of how active or passive you consider her role to be, and use it to respond to the following question: how responsible is Malvonne for the adultery that occurs in her apartment? Do you think the text suggests that she plays an active role in the events that lead to Dorcas's death?

— Think, in more general terms, about the introduction of another member of the community. How does the introduction of characters beyond the triangle of Joe, Violet and Dorcas shift your attitude to the protagonists?

Looking over sections 1–6

QUESTIONS' FOR DISCUSSION OR ESSAYS

1. Discuss the theme of magic in *Jazz*.

2. 'To remember is to re-create.' Discuss, in relation to the opening sections of *Jazz*.

3. Lay out and explain the narrative method of the opening sections of *Jazz*.

4. Consider the themes of trust and betrayal in these opening sections.

SECTION 7 (pp. 53–63)

[This section ends: 'Paradise. All for Paradise'.]

Focus on: the theme of music, and jazz in particular

DETAIL AND EXAMINE . . .

— Throughout this section Alice Manfred talks about different kinds of music. Select the various types of music mentioned. How do her attitudes to different forms of music vary?

— When you have detailed the different kinds of music with which Alice is preoccupied, focus exclusively on jazz and examine her version of it. Think about the following issues:

● How does Alice describe jazz?
● What is her attitude to jazz?
● What moods and emotions does Alice associate with jazz?

LISTEN AND INVESTIGATE . . .

— Listen to some jazz from the period. You might want to read this section while listening to the jazz that Alice is talking about.

— Using the resources provided in the bibliography investigate jazz. See what you can find out about jazz music: what characterises jazz?

EXTEND . . .

— At this point concentrate on broadening your understanding of jazz as a musical genre. Find out what you can about jazz in this period: was it fashionable? Is it described as 'black' music? Reflect upon how important your understanding of jazz music is when considering this novel. See also the exercises in the Contexts section on pp. 133–34.

As you work your way through the text, your analysis will refocus on the relationship of the music to the novel, so keep updating your notes and listening to the music whenever the opportunity arises.

Focus on: language

IDENTIFY SEMANTIC LINKS . . .
The final sentences in this section are 'Paradise. All for Paradise' (p. 63). They refer forward to the third novel in the trilogy and back to the first text.
— As you work your way through the novels, pick out language that links the trilogy. Some phrases are repeated across the three texts. Keep an eye out for such links; jot down phrases that seem familiar and compare the language you have identified to see if it forms a semantic link.

SECTION 8 (pp. 63–73)

Focus on: adolescence

DEFINE AND INTERPRET . . .
— 'By the time she was seventeen her whole life was unbearable' (p. 63). Focus on the first half of this section (pp. 63–7). This is the reader's first real insight into the character of Dorcas. Before going any further, jot down your responses to Dorcas in this incident. However, rather than focusing on her childhood, we – as readers – are given an account of an incident in her adolescence.
— Before turning to the text itself, you need to define what you understand by 'adolescence'. How do you mark the period in an individual's life entitled 'adolescence'? In what ways is it different from 'childhood'? What characteristics define it?
— When you are thinking about the changes that mark adolescence, ensure that you cover the following categories of alteration:

- Physical
- Sexual
- Emotional
- Psychological.

— To what extent is independence an important factor in adolescence?

— When you have worked your way through the various issues suggested above, return to the text and develop the idea of Dorcas as an adolescent here. Use the following questions to help you focus your analysis:

- How does this episode help you to understand the character of Dorcas?
- In terms of your working definition of adolescence, is Dorcas's behaviour here 'adolescent'?
- If Dorcas is an adolescent, what examples in this story illustrate your analysis?

COMPARE AND DISCUSS . . .

— Using your working definition of adolescence and your critical work on Dorcas, think of an incident in your past in which your behaviour was such that you would categorise it as 'adolescent'. In what ways does it fit with your definition?

— Compare and discuss the examples you have chosen. Talk about how they fit your definition.

— When you have discussed your examples, think about your attitude to adolescence. Are you sympathetic to the difficulties of the changes you have identified?

RETURN . . .

— Focusing once more on Dorcas, examine whether or not your attitude to her as a character is more sympathetic when you consider the pressures of adolescence. Would you describe her behaviour in the same way after your discussion of adolescence and the changes it represents?

— As you continue your analysis, think about the extent to which your understanding of Dorcas as an adolescent, or a teenager, influences your attitude to her. Jot down how your expectations of a teenager are different from those of an adult. Keep returning to your notes and question how well Dorcas fits the expectations you have noted.

Focus on: the theme of tragedy

ANALYSE AND INTERPRET . . .

— Look particularly at the second half of this section (pp. 67–73) and the account of Dorcas's and Joe's meeting. This narrative is withheld, creating suspense and heightening expectation.

— Analyse this episode in order to explore how we, as readers, understand Joe and Dorcas at this point. How does this encounter establish the novel's tragedy?

COMPARE . . .

— Use Shakespeare's tragedy *Romeo and Juliet* and compare the specific scene in which Romeo and Juliet meet and fall in love (Act I, scene v) with the meeting of Joe and Dorcas. What similarities do you note in terms of plot and characterisation? Where do the lovers first meet? Is it on purpose or by accident? In public or in private?

— What do you expect from a tragedy, in terms of plot and character? Does *Jazz* fit your expectations: for example, through the tragic separation of the lovers, or simply in the death of a protagonist? Or do both lovers have to die?

EVALUATE . . .

— Through your comparisons, work together to evaluate whether you regard *Jazz* as a tragedy. Think about what makes something a 'tragedy', and how placing *Jazz* within that genre changes your attitude to the novel.

SECTION 9 (pp. 73–82)

Focus on: the theme of fear

CONSIDER . . .

'Toward the end of March, Alice Manfred put her needles aside to think again of what she called the *impunity* of the man who killed her niece just because he could' (p. 73). This opening sentence sets up Alice's thoughts about both Joe and Violet. She talks at length about her fears, both for herself and for the community at large.

— Before you look at this passage in detail, consider what you would expect Alice to be frightened of. Surely Joe Trace, as a murderer, would rate somewhere near the top of her list of concerns? But . . .

— Go back to the passage and pick out the paragraphs that talk about fear: what, in fact, *is* Alice frightened of? How does this section surprise you as she talks about what she is afraid of? In what ways does Morrison refuse to meet your expectations here?

BROADEN . . .

— At various points in this analysis we have focused on how *Jazz* undermines straightforward categories. Widen your interpretation of the theme of fear to think about how the complicated and surprising version of fear ties in with other twists in the novel. To help you focus this exercise you might like to pick one of the following topics, or to assign them individually and then come together in a group to compare your responses:

● How does jazz as a musical style fit with this 'play', and how does it mirror the unexpected turns that this novel takes?

- How do plot twists and diversions create the sense of surprise or instability that you have analysed here?
- How do characters refuse to conform to our expectations of them? (Look back at your analysis of Joe, or forward to questions about Violet.)
- In what ways does the play on common ideas such as 'fear' (and what we expect characters to be afraid of), mirror the novel's destabilisation of the narrative voice?

SECTION 10 (pp. 83–7)

Focus on: the theme of grief

EXAMINE . . .

— 'When Violet came to visit (and Alice never knew when that might be) something opened up' (p. 83). Examine this five-page section, picking out the language that suggests the trauma and grief they feel, such as Alice's assertion 'You don't know what loss is' (p. 87). But also look at how the grief they feel brings these two women together. For instance, look at the distortion of Violet's name in this passage.

ESTABLISH . . .

— Keeping your focus on this, establish how Dorcas's death forms a link between the two women.

— Think about both women being childless and the discussion of this here. How does their separate 'grief' bind them to one another?

— Establish how the women relate to one another through their relationship to the absent Dorcas.

ANALYSE . . .

— Bear in mind, while you are carrying out this analysis, that the women do not grieve for the same things. What else do these women mourn in this conversation, and what do they feel they have lost?

SECTION II (pp. 89–97)

Focus on: language and style

COUNT . . .

— Throughout this passage the narrator employs the phrase '*that* Violet' (p. 90). Work your way through the section and pick out the occurrences of this phrase. How many separate instances of '*that* Violet' are there here?

DETAIL AND DESCRIBE . . .

— Counting the instances focuses your attention on the predominance of a new distinction within the text. What is the distinction that is employed here?

— Think about who '*that* Violet' is. Is there a '*this* Violet'? If she is not indicated, is her presence implicit in the constant reference to '*that*' character?

EVALUATE . . .

— Think closely about the stylistic devices you are noting here. Why do you think the author chooses to put 'that' in italics? How are italics commonly employed? Glance over the pages in this section – if the italics draw your eye, why do you think Morrison wants to capture your attention at this point?

ASSESS . . .

— Select one example of '*that* Violet' and read the context in which it is used (look at the paragraph in which it occurs).

What is the phrase being used to imply here? How does it distance the reader from the action being narrated?

— How does the use of italics here affect your attitude to Violet – does it alter your perception of her? If so, give detailed answers showing how it influences your understanding of Violet.

COMBINE . . .

— Use your analysis of a particular paragraph and compare it with other people's responses. You may have chosen the same instance – if so, how do your readings differ? If you have chosen different examples, are there parallels in your analysis? What ideas link or separate your readings?

— Look both backwards and forwards in the novel for other examples of italicisation. Do these instances work in the same way as the decision to highlight '*that* Violet'?

Looking over sections 7–11

QUESTIONS FOR DISCUSSION OR ESSAYS

1. 'To improvise is to live.' Discuss, in relation to these sections and to the novel as a whole.

2. How is the concept of a 'trilogy' played out in these opening sections?

3. Analyse the treatment of either fear or grief.

SECTION 12 (pp. 97–105)

Focus on: the theme of motherhood

DESCRIBE AND ILLUSTRATE . . .

— 'Sitting in the thin sharp light of the drugstore playing with a long spoon in a tall glass made her think of another woman

. . . her mother' (p. 97). Pick out and describe the events of Violet's childhood as they are told here. Illustrate your description by combining in your response answers to the following questions:

- What happens to her family?
- Who brings the children up?
- What are the different explanations given for Violet's mother's suicide?

EXTEND . . .

The theme of motherhood is important in *Jazz*. For example, not being able to have children is offered as one possible explanation for the creation of *'that* Violet'. (Think about the incident in which Violet attempts to abduct a baby.)
— Taking these examples, develop your analysis of the text by suggesting other places where motherhood is a central thematic concern. You could focus on other characters, such as Felice, Alice or Malvonne. Or you could think about Joe's origins, for his mother plays a crucial role as an embodiment of anti-maternal values. Alternatively you could extend your analysis, but keep the focus solely on Violet, looking at her relationship to both her absent mother and absent children. This would be an assessment of the extent to which Violet is damaged emotionally and psychologically by the absence of the maternal.

COMPARE AND DEVELOP . . .

— When you have developed your thematic analysis of this novel, you might want to extend your critique to the trilogy, in which motherhood forms a central thematic concern. You could contrast the treatment of motherhood in *Beloved* with the analysis you have developed of motherhood in *Jazz*.

Or, if you have looked at *Paradise* initially, you might want to make a comparison between Violet and Mavis, or between Joe's mother and Mavis, if you are interested in the idea of the maternal and what it means to be 'anti-maternal'.

You could even combine all three novels by taking your discussion from Sethe's motherly defence of her children, to Violet's relationship with Dorcas and Mavis's accident.

SECTION 13 (pp. 105–14)

Focus on: the theme of love

DISTINGUISH AND ANALYSE . . .
— Alice gives Violet a piece of advice when Violet asks what she should do, now that Joe has had an affair: '"You want a real thing?" asked Alice. "I'll tell you a real one. You got anything left to you to love, anything at all, do it"' (p. 112). Work through this section looking at the discussion of 'love' that you get here. Pick out the different sorts of love the women talk about. Isolate what distinguishes one type of 'love' from another.
— When you have selected the different types of love these women discuss, look at how Alice presents the idea of love to Violet. How does she suggest to Violet that she needs to think differently about her love for Joe, for example?

ANALYSE . . .
— Using the resources you are provided with in the bibliography consider how ideas about what is attractive complicate these women's idea of love. For example, look at the women's conversation about what makes Dorcas pretty (p. 109). Violet sees Joe's desire for the young woman as compromising her marriage. Does Alice agree?
— Focus on the opening of this section (pp. 105–9). What desire is foregrounded here?

— Think about the following questions:

- How does Violet's desire complicate her relationship to Joe here?
- Does her desire include or exclude Joe?

DISCUSS . . .

— Using the notes you made at the outset of this section, where you selected and analysed various kinds of love, think about these different interpretations of 'love'. How do the desires of Violet and Joe disrupt loving relationships at this point in the text? Do not focus solely on Joe and Violet's relationship; remember that Alice and Dorcas's familial love is disturbed by desire.

— In your discussion encourage one another to be as creative as you can, as you include different characters and facets of the text in your analysis. You may want to make comparisons with other Morrison novels, or extend your discussion to other writers you have studied.

SECTION 14 (pp. 117–29)

This section develops the critical work you did in section 4 of *Jazz*. If you haven't worked on that section yet, you might like to invert the exercise and work through this analysis first, but do combine your analyses for a fuller discussion of the themes and characters examined here.

Focus on: narrative voice

REFRESH . . .

— If you have already worked on section 4, go back and remind yourself of the analysis you performed.

DISTINGUISH . . .

— Divide this section into two parts (pp. 117–21 and 121–9). These two passages are narrated by different narrative voices. Identify what those differences are. Is one a 'first-person narrative' and the other a 'third-person narrative'? Or are they both 'first-person narratives'? (If you are not sure of the meanings of these terms, make sure you discover what they refer to.)

— When you have reached a decision about how you classify the narrative voice, think about who you believe is speaking. Cite evidence from the text to support your claims.

COMPARE AND CONTRAST . . .

— Examine the language of these two passages closely. You may like to work either singly or in pairs, to identify how these narratives operate differently. Below are different interpretative exercises to highlight the literary devices at work in the text:

— How are the narrators stylistically different?

- Count the number of times the narrators identify themselves as 'I' or 'me'; how they refer to characters as 'he', 'she' or 'they'; or whether they use names.
- How do these identifications presume your knowledge as a reader?

— Are you equally familiar with both narrators?

- What contrasts the narrators?
- Produce a character analysis of both narrators at this point to highlight the differences in your knowledge of them.

— Is either of the narrators an 'omniscient narrator'?

- Rewrite a paragraph changing the narrative voice.
- How does this influence the tone of your paragraph?
- Does it, in fact, alter the information given here about characters or setting?
- Do you have to make assumptions; do you become the author of a new text?

— Look at the textual differences you have noted in these sections, then use this evidence as a basis for your response to the following questions: how do you react differently to a first person speaking directly to you? How does your attitude to the speaker act as a filter to what they say? Do we, as readers, regard third-person narrators as more reliable than individual voices? If so, why?

Focus on: Joe Trace

CHARACTERISE . . .
— Analyse the character of Joe, based on the account you are given here of his childhood. Make sure that you include in your discussion consideration of issues such as:

- Abandonment
- Naming
- Fraternity
- Hunting.

— You may decide that you want to work through each issue under a sub-heading, but bring these facets of Joe's character together to focus on the notion of identity. How does Joe characterise these issues as creating his identity?

COMBINE . . .
— Link your earlier analysis (see section 5) with this discus-

sion of the formation of Joe's identity. How does your increased knowledge of his childhood inform your attitude to Joe and his murder of Dorcas?

SECTION 15 (pp. 130–5)

Focus on: the theme of hunting

EXAMINE AND CRITIQUE . . .
— This sub-section opens with an account of Dorcas's acne: 'Little half moons clustered underneath her cheekbones, like faint hoofmarks' (p. 130). Examine Joe's account of her, and his attempts to locate her, as an extended metaphor. Select the phrases that link his narrative to hunting, then critique the literary device. How does the use of the metaphor create a sense of Dorcas's fate? Does the metaphorical use of hunting alter your perception of her? Does it change your attitude to Joe?
— Think about your critique of this extended metaphor and use it to produce an essay-style answer to the following questions: how does the extended metaphor of hunting challenge your understanding of Dorcas's death? Is the relationship of the hunter to prey different from that of the murderer and victim?

Focus on: the theme of perfection

DISCOVER AND INTERPRET . . .
— Joe describes Dorcas in the following terms: 'I told you again that you were the reason Adam ate the apple and its core' (p. 133). If you have never done so, you might like to read the story of Adam and Eve in Genesis in the Old Testament of the Bible. Establish your knowledge of the story itself.
— Look particularly at this page of text and think about the idea of 'Eden' (p. 133). How is the idea of perfection undermined

in Dorcas and Joe's relationship? You may like to spend some time thinking about the idea of the Fall, as referred to here. Think about how well Joe and Dorcas parallel the icons in terms of succumbing to desire. Also, consider the characters' relationship to good and evil as set out in these terms – is there a satanic figure lurking to tempt 'Eve/Dorcas'?

EXTEND . . .

— When you have worked with these two texts you may want to tie your analysis into *Paradise*, as there is clearly an inter-textual reference here. Depending upon the depth of analysis that you are attempting, you might like to look at other texts that famously consider the concept of Eden, such as *Paradise Lost* (1667) by John Milton or *Utopia* (1516) by Thomas More. (For a fuller discussion of 'Eden', see the part of this book that considers the third novel in the trilogy, *Paradise*, especially pp. 189–191.)

SECTION 16 (pp. 137–55)

Focus on: style and structure

DETERMINE AND CHARACTERISE . . .

— As a novel, *Jazz* has a complex structure. At this point the focus shifts from 1920s' New York to a different time period and location. Use the information you are given here to deter-mine the context of this portion of the narrative. When you are clear about the location and period, use the list below to characterise this excerpt of the text:

- Flash-back
- History
- Biography
- Autobiography

- Memoir
- Myth
- Fairy story.

Before you finalise a choice, you might like to discuss what you believe differentiates these categories. For example, what is the difference between an autobiography and a memoir? You may want to alter or combine terms, or reject the list entirely and establish your own.

REFLECT . . .

— Think about your choice and its implications. Could it be extended to the novel as a whole? If you chose 'memoir', is *Jazz* a 'memoir'? Reflect on the complexity of categorising the novel as a whole. Why is this difficult to do?

— Concentrate on the idea of a complicated narrative. What demands are made on the reader in this novel? Do they shift, depending on the section of text you are working with?

Focus on: the theme of colour

RESEARCH . . .

— This chapter sets up a complex discussion of race and colour-line racism. Begin your analysis by establishing your own understanding of the terms. Some of these terms occur within the novel (for example, 'mulatto'), while others inform the debate. Take each of the terms listed below and establish their meaning:

- Mulatto
- Negro
- Octoroon
- The 'One Drop Rule'
- Miscegenation.

ESTABLISH AND EVALUATE . . .

— When you have established the terms' individual meanings consider the implications of this set of phrases. How many of these terms were familiar to you?

— Consider the consequences of defining individuals in terms of their colour and their relationship to 'whiteness' and 'blackness'. How do these terms affect your understanding of yourself? How does the use of these formal categories constrict identity? Refer to Morrison's comments on this question in the interview on pp. 12–13.

RETURN AND EXAMINE . . .

— When you have considered this new vocabulary, focus your attention back on this section of text. Pick out the different references to colour given here. For example, how is the pregnant woman described? How many different descriptions of her blackness are given? How is the protagonist of this section entitled?

— How is your attitude to these descriptions influenced by your analysis of the vocabulary of colour-line racism? How does Morrison manipulate the characterisation of individuals through the hue of their skin? How is her employment of colour used to empower or disempower characters?

INTERROGATE . . .

— Building on your critique of the language of colour, look exclusively at the character of 'Golden Gray' (p. 139). Unpack Golden Gray as an example of Morrison's discussion of identifications and assumptions made on the grounds of colour. In order to interrogate him thoroughly, use the following pointers to help you in your analysis:

- What does it mean to be 'Golden'?
- Why is he named as he is?

- What does he associate with dark colours? (Look at his comparison of the wild woman and his horse.)
- What does whiteness symbolise here? (Draw up a list of what Golden believes it represents.)
- How is he both a perpetrator of colour distinctions and a victim of them?

EXTEND . . .

— Take this sophisticated analysis of colour and think about its consequences for the novel as a whole. For example, you might like to consider the relationship of whiteness to beauty by looking at the products that Joe buys and Dorcas sells. Or you might want to extend your analysis of descriptions of blackness throughout the novel.

SECTION 17 (pp. 155–62)

Focus on: the theme of loss

ANALYSE AND INTERPRET . . .

— Golden Gray muses here about his father: 'Only now, he thought, now that I know I have a father, do I feel his absence' (p. 158). Analyse his treatment of loss here. How does he describe his sense of love? What metaphors and similes does he use? In what ways does his account surprise you – are any elements of it unexpected? (Look particularly at the rest of the sentence quoted here.)

RELATE . . .

— Golden's account of his sense of loss suggests the idea of physical pain, and a permanent difference in his perception of himself. Think about a particular memory that evokes such a strong sense of feeling within you (it does not have to be loss;

it could be anger, love or even something funny) and try to write a short account of it.

— You may want to get together and compare narratives, or you may prefer to discuss the difficulties you face as a writer. How difficult is it to frame a particular feeling so as to reflect the exact response that it evokes in you?

— When discussing your attempts, focus in depth on how language sometimes makes expression more difficult, as opposed to clarifying feelings. For example, did you end up wanting to say, 'You had to be there'?

ASSESS . . .

— Reread this section of the novel. How does your attempt at conveying a defining emotion alter your perspective on Golden's account? Does it increase your sense of intimacy with Golden, or does it remind you of the complexity of constructing the apparently 'natural' feelings of a character?

Looking over sections 12–17

QUESTIONS FOR DISCUSSION OR ESSAYS

1.   'To be a mother is to give and to lose.' Discuss, with reference to *Jazz*.

2.   Analyse and explain the different kinds of love portrayed in the novel so far.

3.   'Paradise can only exist in fairy tale and in the imagination.' Discuss, with reference to *Jazz*.

4.   Consider Morrison's treatment of the theme of colour in the novel so far.

5.   What connections can you make at this point in your reading between Morrison's *Jazz* and her earlier novel, *Beloved?*

SECTION 18 (pp. 165–73)

Focus on: the theme of natural versus wild

DETAIL AND DEVELOP . . .
This chapter opens with a consideration of Joe Trace's mother at his birth: 'Any fascination could mark a newborn: melons, rabbits, wisteria, rope, and, more than a shed snakeskin, a wild woman is the worst of all.' (p. 165). Throughout this passage Morrison establishes and manipulates the idea of the 'natural'.
— Read through this part of the text and pick out the language of nature that is used here. What is being described by these phrases? Is the narrator actually referring to the environment, or are these terms being used to describe characters, as in the example above.

DELINEATE AND DISTINGUISH . . .
— Having looked closely for the natural language used in this section, explore the differences between the idea of something 'natural' and the characteristics of 'wildness'. Start by jotting down the associations you make with the terms – for example, we frequently associate wildness with danger, but not necessarily with nature. How are our expectations different when we read these terms?
— Turn your attention back to the text and see if Morrison employs the distinction between the wild and the natural so as to fit your expectations of the terms.

RE-INTRODUCE . . .
— Taking your analysis of the idea of the 'natural' as opposed to the 'wild', re-introduce your focus to the idea of the 'Hunter' (see section 15). How does the role of the hunter mediate between the natural and the wild? (Think both about

the environment and in terms of behaviour, which is often characterised as 'normal behaviour', or 'wild behaviour'.)

— Use your discussion of the hunter as someone who tames the wilderness, or makes it 'natural', and incorporate it into your character analysis of Joe. How is Joe tied to the idea of the 'wild' through the women to whom he is connected? (Think both about the treatment of his mother here and of Violet's 'wild' behaviour in the City.)

SECTION 19 (pp. 173–84)

Focus on: the theme of memory

ASSESS . . .

— Pay particular attention to the framing pages of this excerpt (pp. 173–4 and 181–4), and examine the treatment of memory here. How is your attitude to Joe's attempts to meet his mother influenced by the explicit references to memory at the opening of the section?

— Assess the extent to which Joe's memories become confused. Can you clearly separate his memories of hunting Dorcas from his attempts to find his mother? How does the confusion affect your confidence in his version of events?

LINK AND COMPARE . . .

— The unreliability of the narrative voice has been highlighted as a thematic concern in *Jazz*. In your assessment of memory you have looked at issues concerning the unreliability of the narrator's version of events. Combine your discussion of memory with the idea of the unreliable narrator and think about how memories form the foundation of this novel. As you link your analysis of memory with narrative voice, use these questions to stimulate comparison:

- Do you consider memory to be a reliable resource?
- How much of this novel consists of the recounting of memories?
- Think about the use of the present tense. Are narrators really present, or do they recollect incidents *as if* they were occurring?

Focus on: the theme of family

EVALUATE . . .

— Turn your attention to Joe's description of his mother. In what ways does his relationship with his mother refuse to conform to the usual model of the family? Start with basic assumptions about the family unit. You might like to look up the dictionary definition of 'family' and think about how Joe's family unit forms the antithesis to this.

EXTEND . . .

— Joe's relationship with his mother undermines a simplistic understanding of what it means to be part of a family, or to have a straightforward relationship between a mother and her son. Extend your analysis of the disruption of family structures to consider other family units in *Jazz*. Are there, in fact, any 'normal' families in this text?

— Come back to this question at the end of your analysis. How does the set-up between Felice, Joe and Violet support or undermine the simple or 'nuclear' family model (Dad, Mum and 2.4 children)?

ASSESS . . .

— You may want to combine your work on this section with your thoughts on the 'natural' in the previous section. If these family constructs are not simple, does that stop them being 'natural'? Consider the idea of the nuclear family. Is it one that you believe in, or do you have a more sophisticated version of what it means to be a member of a family? Is the traditional family model in fact one that includes grandparents, aunts and uncles as integral members of the family? Is isolating 'Mum and Dad' as the adult family unit in fact unnatural?

RELATE . . .
— Think about taking this discussion of the family one stage further, and go back to your analysis of distinctions of colour (section 16). Combine your analysis of the family with your consideration of identifications made on the grounds of colour, by responding to the following statement: there are no 'natural' families in *Jazz* because unnatural distinctions – identifying individuals in relation to their colour – make this impossible. (You may want to work alone, in pairs or as a group. Write up your responses so that you have to formalise your ideas about the question.)

SECTION 20 (pp. 187–93)

Focus on: desire and being desired

CONCEPTUALISE . . .
— Dorcas talks us through her romance with Acton here. How would you describe their relationship? What kinds of desire is it based upon? (Think about Acton and Joe's desires, as well as Dorcas's.) Use the suggestions of different aspects of desire below to focus your analysis:

- Sexual desire
- Social approval
- Jealousy
- Cruelty
- Greed

● Maturity.

— How do different desires overlap here (for example, Dorcas's keenness to be desired as an adult with her desire to hurt Joe)?

INFER . . .
— Through your analysis of desire, think about how Dorcas's yearning to be desired by both Acton and Joe defines her at this point in the story.

SECTION 21 (pp. 195–8)

Focus on: mood and tone

CONTRAST . . .
— 'Sweetheart' (p. 195). What is being described in this opening word? How does the subject of this description take the reader by surprise?
— Look at the description of the weather and think about the context of this section. Examine the construction of the mood at this point. Is the tone full of foreboding? Does the weather prepare us for the events that take place on this day?
— Analyse Morrison's juxtaposition of the events and their context through the establishment of mood and tone here. Be specific in your selection of the phrases that set the tone at this point.

EXPLORE . . .
— Think about the consequences of the tone you have identified. How does it disrupt the course of the text? Does it destabilise the reader by refusing to conform to a particular pattern? What might you expect the tone and mood to be in the build-up to Dorcas's murder?

— How does this surprise, in terms of mood and tone, parallel the destabilisation of the narrative voice in the novel? How does it help the attempt to stop the novel having a single authoritative tone?

SECTION 22 (pp. 198–206)

Focus on: the character of Felice versus Dorcas

COMPARE AND CONTRAST . . .

— 'Dorcas was my friend, but I knew that in a way she was right . . . Dorcas was a fool, but when I met the old man I sort of understood' (p. 206). Work your way through this section and pay close attention to Felice's account of Dorcas. How does she set herself up in opposition to Dorcas? What differences are highlighted between the two girls? Think also about how they are linked – what sympathies and interests do they share?

CONSIDER . . .

— Having looked at the two characters, and their similarities and differences, think about how they are combined through language. Look at the language that connects them – what phrases link the two women? Who is speaking, and are they speaking directly about the other girl? How does this link them together?

EXTEND . . .

— Now develop your analysis of Dorcas and Felice's meeting to consider how they are connected thematically. Look particularly at the account of the ring in this passage. How are the girls linked by themes such as parents, desire and isolation?
— Think about how the girls work together to form a single identity in the minds of others. You may find it particularly

useful to continue thinking about the thematic, linguistic and characteristic links between the two girls as you work your way through the next section of the text.

SECTION 23 (pp. 207–15)

Focus on: the theme of happiness

RESEARCH AND REFLECT . . .
—— 'I've seen him smile twice now and laugh out loud once' (p. 207). Discover what the name 'Felice' means. How is her name important here, in terms of her interaction with Joe and Violet?
—— When you have established its meaning, think about happiness in this section of the novel. How do we convey to others that we are 'happy', and how does Morrison suggest to us that the Trace family is happy here?

REASSESS . . .
—— When you have analysed the section for suggestions of happiness, think about how this is qualified. It is not a straightforward happy ending, so pick out what complicates the happiness that Felice notes.
—— You may want to relate to your discussion of the similarities between Dorcas and Felice (section 22), if you attempted that analysis. If not, think about whether or not Felice replaces other absent characters: Dorcas, the children Joe and Violet never had. Is this what forms the substance of the happy ending, or what undermines it?

Focus on: language, communication and dialogue

PERFORM . . .
—— Get together in a group, assign characters and read out the extended dialogue of this section (pp. 208–15).

DETERMINE . . .

— Now, in the groups you have formed, discuss what effect hearing the dialogue read aloud has had upon you. Has it altered your perception of individual characters? Or does it make you think differently about the context as a whole?

ANALYSE . . .

— Using your discussion as a base, think about dialogue here. How does it suggest 'communication'? Start with literal responses, but extend your argument to consider both the act of speaking and the idea of communicating thoughts and emotions. Use the following questions to aid your analysis:

- How does the dialogue suggest that Violet and Joe are becoming close once again?
- Does Felice mediate between the couple and, if so, how is this suggested in the dialogue? (Focus on the role of the listener or understanding figure.)
- Where is the reader placed? How are we involved in the dialogue and the idea of communication and understanding?

Focus on: the theme of music, and jazz in particular

REVIEW OR LISTEN . . .

— In section 7 you were asked to consider the importance of jazz music to the novel. If the exercise is one that you selected then, look over your notes to remind yourself of the ideas you formed. If that section is not one you focused on, then you may want to familiarise yourself with the genre. Make sure that you listen to some jazz from the period so that you have a feel for the music that is being referred to. You might refer to Morrison's comments on jazz in the interview on p. 15.

RELATE . . .

— Felice offers to bring around records after they hear music drifting in from another apartment. Use your previous work on *Jazz* to think about the function of music in this section. Look at its association with liberation and intimacy. What does it symbolise at this point in the narrative?

COMBINE . . .

— You may want to combine your responses with your discussion of happiness. Or you could contrast Alice's reaction to jazz with the Traces' joy at the re-introduction of music to the home. Alternatively, you could reconsider your attitude to the title of the novel. How is *Jazz* informed by the narrative's incorporation of music at this point?

SECTION 24 (pp. 215–16)

Focus on: the theme of motherhood

ANALYSE AND INTERPRET . . .

— Look closely at Felice's account of her mother here. Pay particular attention to the final paragraph: 'her catfish was pretty good' (p. 216). How does she align her understanding in relation to Violet? Think about the different maternal relationships you are presented with here – how do the different women to whom Felice refers complicate a simple definition of 'motherhood'?

EXTEND . . .

— Extend your analysis of motherhood to incorporate your work on the text as a whole. (You may want to link it directly to your analysis of section 12.)

— Think about the number of maternal roles that you notice in this text which do not concern mothers and daughters. How

is the idea of motherhood complicated by the relationships
that you focus on?

TRACE . . .

— The following list suggests some of the focal characters in
terms of debates about motherhood. Map out the interrelationships. Who is whose mother – who plays a maternal role
for whom? Whose mothers are absent? Whose maternal fig-
ures are not included in the list below?

- Violet
- Rose Dear
- True Belle
- Golden Gray
- Joe Trace
- Wild woman
- Felice
- Dorcas
- Alice
- Malvonne
- Felice's mother
- Felice's grandmother.

— Use the list and either focus on one or two characters or
combine them in a more sweeping analysis to respond to these
statements:

- *Jazz* reworks the idea of the maternal.
- To be a mother on biological grounds is exploded as a justification for the title of 'Mum'.
- The role of the 'mother', however, is highlighted as a fundamental need – a source of identification – for all
  individuals.
- The maternal is the central parental relationship in *Jazz*,

but the paternal precipitates the crisis that results in Dorcas's death.

You may want to respond orally or on paper, but if you decide to talk through the issues, make sure that you keep good notes as this is one of the novel's central concerns.

SECTION 25 (pp. 219–29)

Focus on: the theme of movement

EVALUATE . . .

— 'There was an evening, back in 1906, before Joe and Violet went to the City, when Violet left the plow and walked into their little shotgun house' (p. 225). Throughout your analysis you have looked at various kinds of physical, emotional and psychological journeys. Think about movement at the end of the novel. How is the sense of journey, travel and movement brought to a halt here?

EXAMINE IN PARTICULAR . . .

— Think about the final description: 'When I see them now they are not sepia, still losing their edges . . . For me they are real. Sharply in focus and clicking' (p. 226). How does the metaphor of the photograph relate to the sense of movement? Does it suggest something static, or a glimpse of a particular movement?

INTEGRATE . . .

— Re-introduce other ideas that you have had about movement; look over your notes – you may want to pick up on ideas of hunting, journeys or even the movement of music as it travels up and down the scale.

— Would you want to characterise the novel as 'active'? If so, why?

Focus on: narrative structure

ASSESS . . .

— 'But I can't say that aloud; . . . Say make me, remake me. You are free to do it and I am free to let you because look, look. Look where your hands are. Now' (p. 229). At various points in your analysis the importance of the narrative voice has been highlighted. Think about this ending, and how this unknown narrator frames the text.

QUESTION . . .

— In order to bring your analysis full circle, think about the following questions in relation to this final section, and particularly the end of the novel:

● At this point are we, as readers, any closer to knowing who is speaking?
● If not, are we still trying to discover their identity?
● Do we trust this individual? Are they consistent? Give examples to support your discussion either way.
● Would you be able to construct a character analysis of them at this point?
● Do we read the narrator as Morrison? Defend your response.
● Morrison actively seeks to destabilise the authority of the narrative voice. How does the end of the novel support this?

REFLECT . . .

— Use the above questions as a way of combining previous analyses. Think about the ending – you may want to reconsider questions raised here about the idea of happiness and motherhood.

— Take the issues that most interest you and think about how your attitude has altered to the themes and issues you focused on.

Looking over sections 18–25

QUESTIONS FOR DISCUSSION OR ESSAYS

1. Consider the comparison between the 'natural' and the 'wild' in these sections.

2. How does Morrison use the idea of memory?

3. Analyse the use of the first and third persons in these sections.

Looking back over the whole novel

QUESTIONS FOR DISCUSSION OR ESSAYS

1. Why is 'Trace' an important name in this novel?

2. Examine the theme of jazz and explain the influence of this music on the narrative method of the novel as a whole.

3. Explain the connections between *Jazz* and *Beloved* in terms of plot, imagery and language.

4. Consider the image of the city as portrayed in *Jazz*.

5. 'This is not a story to pass on.' (*Beloved* p. 275) Write about stories and storytelling in *Jazz*.

Contexts, comparisons and complementary readings

JAZZ

Context is important for the three novels in this trilogy. Many of the contextual suggestions made here expand on contexts touched upon within the detailed reading guides. If you have looked at the more contextual exercises already suggested, then use them as a springboard for this fuller discussion. If you didn't look at those facets of the novel, then this section provides an opportunity to fully explore contextual and comparative analytic tools.

These sections suggest contextual and comparative ways of reading these three novels by Morrison. You can put your reading in a social, historical or literary context. You can make comparisons – again, social, literary or historical – with other texts. Or you can choose complementary works (of whatever kind) – that is, works of art, literary works, social reportage or facts that illuminate the text, by giving a framework to references that you currently find oblique. Some of the suggested contexts are directly connected to the books, in that they give you precise literary or social frames within which to situate the novel. In turn, these are either related to the period within which the novel is set, or to the time – now – when you are reading it. Some of these examples are designed to suggest books or other texts that may make useful sources for comparison (or for complementary purposes) when you are reading *Jazz*. Again, they may be related to literary or critical themes, or they may be relevant to social and cultural themes current 'then' or 'now'.

Also, bear in mind the nature of a trilogy. Your contextual research for one of the texts will prove extremely useful in your work on the others. Equally, by reference to the themes that run throughout the trilogy, be aware that your analysis of individual texts could be used to inform another text. For example, here your research encourages a consideration of motherhood, which reappears with a slightly different focus in both *Beloved* and *Paradise*. You might want to bring these discussions together to give you an overall response to the trilogy.

Focus on: jazz music

RESEARCH AND LISTEN . . .

— The period in which this novel is written is known as the Harlem Renaissance. Using texts such as *Black Culture and the Harlem Renaissance* (1988) by Cary Wintz or *The Harlem Renaissance, a Historical Dictionary for the Era* (1984) by Bruce Kellner, and the Internet, discover what you can about the Harlem Renaissance. It is often treated as a significant historical moment in terms of black cultural emancipation. Use the knowledge you are accruing to aid your evaluation of the period.

— Why do you think Morrison chooses to set *Jazz* in the Harlem Renaissance? It does not explicitly make up the focus of the novel, so how does this context alter your attitude to *Jazz*? What does it establish in terms of black history? Use the

Morrison interview to inform your responses. (You may want to think about the extension of historical context here. How is Morrison tracing a particular black history in the transition from slave narratives to Harlem Renaissance?)

— Now tailor your research to look specifically at jazz music in the Harlem Renaissance. Listen to some jazz from the period. Using reference texts – for example, *The New Grove Dictionary of Jazz* edited by Barry Kernfeld (1988) or *The Guinness Jazz Companion* by Peter Clayton and Peter Gammond (1989) – or more specific texts, such as Samuel Floyd Jr's *Black Music in the Harlem Renaissance, A Collection of Essays* (1990), detail the qualities that define the genre. Focus particularly on the idea of improvisation: think about how the qualities of the music inform the narrative.

Focus on: maternal origins

RESEARCH AND COMPARE . . .

— As a writer, Morrison is often compared to William Faulkner. The female line is a serious concern in both *Jazz* and Faulkner's *Absalom, Absalom!* (1936). For instance, focus on Golden Gray and Joe Trace, and then compare them with the unfolding incestuous narrative at the heart of Faulkner's novel.

— Compare the treatment of the complexity of origins displayed here. You may wish to tie this in with the historical research you have conducted as part of your analysis of *Jazz*, or even that undertaken in your work on *Beloved*. How do anxieties about blood-line influence this discussion of maternality?

— In *Jazz* motherhood is treated more in terms of breeding. Look at Lisa Jardine's *Still Harping on Daughters: Women and Drama in the Age of Shakespeare* (1983). Think about how the concern to keep a 'pure' blood-line is more of a consideration for Golden Gray than a desire to know his absent mother.

Focus on: mental health

COMPARE AND CONTRAST . . .

— In *Jazz*, Violet clearly experiences a breakdown. Look at other textual treatments of mental illness and think about how a psychological breakdown is conveyed in narratives. Novels such as Virginia Woolf's *Mrs Dalloway* (1925) and Kate Chopin's *The Awakening* (1899) provide literary precedents. Or (extending the comparison with Faulkner suggested in the preceding focus, as well as in the contextualisation of *Beloved* on p. 83) you could read the opening section of his work *The Sound and the Fury* (1929). For a contemporary comparison you could look at the novels of Toni Cade Bambara, such as *Gorilla My Love* (1972) or *The Sea Birds Are Still Alive* (1972), or at the prize-winning novel by Toi Derricote entitled *The Black Notebooks* (1997).

— Look at the narrative and linguistic techniques that these writers employ to suggest mental illness. For example, Morrison employs an internal distinction through her use of the phrase '*that* Violet' (p. 90). Faulkner suggests a collapse in the dimension of time. Both Morrison and Derricote employ a linguistic fragmentation, refusing to convey their narrative in fully constructed sentences.

INTEGRATE . . .

— Combine your work on the collapse of a coherent identity with the idea of the crises that women (particularly Violet and Dorcas) face in *Jazz*. Think about the gendering of mental breakdown: with the exception of Faulkner, the writers mentioned above deal with the collapse of female consciousness. Look at the demands that pressurise these women, forcing them to question what gives them value as individuals.

DISCUSS . . .

— Talk about the pressures that these novels identify. Do

they vary significantly? Compare for example, the Chopin as opposed to Derricote? Are these still psychological pressures that we recognise today? Do we need them to be clinically defined in order to recognise their force? For example, are we, as a society, more sympathetic to the idea of postnatal depression, than we are to Violet's gut-splitting desire for a child?

Focus on: the City

DISCOVER, MAP AND EXPLORE . . .

— Throughout *Jazz* New York is described as 'the City' (p. 10). Look at Toni Morrison's own discussion 'City Limits Village Values' and at histories of New York, or at a more general account of American history with chapters that consider black New York specifically (such as *The Harvard Guide to African American History*), to develop an understanding of the novel's setting. Look at images of the city at this period to give you a sense of the layout to which Morrison refers.

— Think about specific questions, such as:

- What is the El? (Chicago's El still remains, so you might want to think about how it influences our view of a city. If you do not regard it as iconic, just watch one episode of *ER*!)
- What is a shotgun house?
- What is Tiffany's? Develop your understanding by thinking about the cultural status of 'Tiffany's'. If you can, watch *Breakfast at Tiffany's*, directed by Blake Edwards (1961), and contrast the version of non-white New Yorkers (epitomised by Mickey Rooney) with Felice's account of segregation. How does the solely white cast support Felice's account of the City? (Mickey Rooney plays a Chinese neigh-

bour to Audrey Hepburn, because Paramount was not prepared to cast an oriental actor in the role.)

CONCEPTUALISE . . .
— Take your investigation of New York and consider what is represented culturally and socially by the idea of a city representing a) a geographical area b) a mood c) a way of life d) a certain type of character or personality and e) a nation. What might it mean to be a 'New Yorker'? How would you interpret a statement like 'She's so New York'? How is the idea of New York seen to epitomise a Nation at its best? You could contrast London to New York or you could focus entirely upon the Big Apple, think about texts such as Theodore Dreiser's *Sister Carrie* (1900), the original American Novel, or contemporary films such as *The Matrix* or *Spiderman*. They may be nominally located somewhere else, but the locations are identifiable as the Capital or as a major city with a particular character. How does Morrison convey the partiality of this vision in her treatment of 'the City'? Contrast these films with her version of Harlem, what it cannot offer its inhabitants and how they are refused access to 'the City' itself.

VINTAGE
LIVING
TEXTS

Paradise

IN CLOSE-UP

Reading guides for

PARADISE

BEFORE YOU BEGIN TO READ . . .
— Read the interview with Morrison. You will see there that she identifies a number of themes:

- Love
- Storytelling
- Women and men.

Other themes that it may be useful to consider while reading the novel include:

- Desire
- Ambiguity
- Death.

Reading activities: detailed analysis

DEDICATION AND EPIGRAPH

Focus on: quotations

ANALYSE . . .

— Spend some time focusing on the epigraph with which Morrison opens the novel. Concentrate on the language used. How would you characterise the quotation? Do you regard it as a poem, an excerpt from a novel, a biblical citation? Which particular words and phrases led you to your choice?

— What themes do you think this citation establishes for the novel? Do they tie in with your focus on the title? How do the title and this quotation set up particular expectations for *Paradise*? Keep coming back to your expectations as you work your way through the novel – are they met as you read, or are you surprised by the thematic concerns you perceive it to focus on?

INVESTIGATE . . .

— When you have considered the material, you might like to conduct some research into the origin of the quotation. What comes before and after this citation – what is its context?

— How does your knowledge of the quotation's origin and context affect your predictions for the themes of this text?

Have they been supported by your research or would you want
to reconsider their focus?

COMPARE AND CONTRAST . . .
— If you are working on the novels as a trilogy you may want
to compare and contrast the framing quotations that Morrison
uses for the three novels. Think first about the difference in
presentation: why, for example, does she give sources for the
Beloved and *Jazz* quotations, but not for the *Paradise* one?
— How is your attitude to the quotations dictated by what
you know about the context of what is being cited?

EXTEND . . .
— When you have considered the different ways in which
these quotations frame the texts you are studying think about
why Morrison chooses to open the novels with citations.
— Also bear in mind the ways in which these three novels
resurface in each other. If you want to explore the relationship of the three novels to one another more extensively, work
through the section of this book devoted to the trilogy on
pp. 20–3.

RUBY
SECTION 1 (pp. 3–4)

Focus on: ambiguity

LIST . . .
— 'They shoot the white girl first' (p. 3) is the opening sen-
tence of *Paradise*. Before extending your analysis, stop and scru-
tinise this statement.
— Think about the ways in which this sentence is ambiguous.
What do you need to know in order to make sense of this

statement? Working solely on this opening, list the information you need in order to fully understand this sentence's meaning. For example:

- Object – you need to establish who the object of the sentence is (the white girl referred to)
- Subject – 'they' is non-specific (it tells you nothing about who is doing the shooting).

— In fact, although this statement seems relatively transparent, it gives you very little information. Use your list to establish a context for this statement: what will the text need to inform you about for you to be able to fully comprehend the implications of this opening?

EXAMINE AND DESCRIBE . . .

— Now turn your attention to this section as a whole (pp. 3–4). Work your way closely through this passage, picking out the details you are given. Does it provide you with a context for the opening sentence – are you told who the object and subject of the shooting are?

— When you have gleaned the information you are provided with in this section, look at the construction of the sentences which have given you that information. How would you describe them: are they long or short? Complex or simple?

— Keeping your focus on the structure of this section, look at the final paragraph, starting 'Outside, the mist is waist high.' (p. 4) Look first at the language used: which of the words or phrases are unfamiliar to you? What are the 'grass rainbows' that are referred to?

— Then think about the deliberate ambiguities in this paragraph: who are the 'witches' that will have left the tracks?

CONSIDER . . .

— Bring together your analysis of this section as a whole, and think about the idea of ambiguity.

— First, establish what you understand it to mean — give examples of what you would normally consider to be an ambiguous phrase or statement.

— Second, think about whether the language you have studied here fits in with your examples. When you first read this opening were you struck by its ambiguity, or did it initially appear to be direct and clear in its linguistic construction?

— Third, consider ambiguity as a narrative tool. How does it manipulate the reader? What questions does it encourage the reader to ask of the text? How important are ambiguities or mysteries for the reader? Do they affect what you pay attention to as you analyse this opening section?

REFRESH . . .

— Do you ever discover which of the women at 'the Convent' (p. 3) is 'the white girl'? If not, think about how the creation of that ambiguity affects your reading.

— Keep focusing on the idea of textual ambiguity as you work your way through the novel. Bear in mind that being ambiguous doesn't necessarily mean being vague or indirect — something may appear straightforward without actually informing you of anything.

— Return to the idea of ambiguity as your reading develops, thinking about how it affects your interpretation of the novel's thematic concerns. For example, how does refusing to solve certain mysteries stop the reader from jumping to conclusions about characters? What is the relationship between the text's ambiguities and the theme of judgement in the novel?

RUBY
SECTION 2 (pp. 5–12)

Focus on: the Convent versus Ruby

MAP . . .

— Use the details you are provided with to construct a map of the Convent. Determine the layout of the building, and the location of the characters within it. Trace the journey of the men throughout the space, and ensure that your map indicates not only the space of the Convent, but also what the men describe in the rooms as they work their way through it. Morrison talks in the interview (on p. 17) about the care she takes over such detail.

HISTORICISE . . .

— When you have mapped out the space of the Convent, look over this section for the history of the building. What are you told here about the Convent and its origin?

— Are you given a history of the town of 'Ruby' here? Compare the description of the Convent with your historicisation of Ruby. How is Ruby set up in relation to the Convent at this early point in the narrative? Think about the following oppositions and expand on them using this section of text:

● Female v. male
● Salvation v. sin
● Community v. individuals.

— Create oppositions of your own and think about how the text challenges them. Do you want to put Ruby or the Convent on both sides of these oppositions – if so, why?

— Update your notes on the history of Ruby and the Convent.

How are they contrasted to one another in terms of the developing history you are given for both locations?

RUBY
SECTION 3 (pp. 12–18)

Focus on: the theme of brothers

CHARACTERISE . . .

— Look at the treatment of the brothers in this section. Draw up a character study of the two men. What are you told about their physical, emotional and psychological characters here?

EXPLORE . . .

— Work together and think about other famous literary examples of brothers. Draw up your own list of examples and, using that think about the literary heritage of brotherhood. Consider, for instance:

- Cain and Abel
- Old Hamlet and Claudius
- Joseph and his brothers (*Genesis* chapters 37–50).

— What thematic links do you identify at this point between the examples you chose to consider and your analysis of the twins?

MAVIS
SECTION 1 (pp. 21–32)

Focus on: the theme of motherhood

LIST . . .

— 'The neighbors seemed pleased when the babies smothered' (p. 21). Look at the treatment of maternity in this chapter. Start by sketching out the different maternal relationships you are given here. Think about how many generations they span, focusing particularly on Mavis and her position as both mother and child.

DISCUSS . . .

— When you have teased out the different versions of motherhood that you are given here, get into groups and discuss your conception of what it means to be a 'mother'. What words and phrases define your understanding of the term?

INTERROGATE. . .

— Turn your attention back to this section of text and question your definition of 'motherhood'. Use the following questions as starting points for your analysis:

● How does Mavis fit, in terms of your definition?
● Does Mavis's version of events contradict your comprehension of the twins' death?
● How does Mavis's reaction to her other children affect your attitude to her as a mother?

— Look at Mavis's mother's behaviour. How does it sit with your discussion of motherhood?

ASSESS . . .

— Think about your assessment of motherhood. Has your attitude to Mavis changed as you have conducted your analysis? Do you think our expectations of 'mothers' make us harder as readers on Mavis, or is our sympathy aroused by the idea of a mother losing her children?

EXTEND . . .

— As you analyse the rest of 'Mavis' and the novel, think about the other mothers you come across. The theme of motherhood is highlighted again, but crops up throughout the text. Update your notes as you encounter other versions of the theme. (You may want to extend this discussion to include both *Beloved* and *Jazz* – see the section on the trilogy on pp. 21–4.)

MAVIS
SECTION 2 (pp. 32–42)

Focus on: the theme of journeys

DETERMINE . . .

— Find a map of the United States of America and trace Mavis's journey from Maryland to New Jersey and Oklahoma. Familiarise yourself with the geography, and the sheer length of the journey. Mavis narrates her route so that you can specifically trace the journey of the Cadillac.

COMPARE . . .

— Think about a road journey that you are familiar with. It may be a personal experience or a fictional example, such as Jack Kerouac's *On the Road* (1957) or the film *Thelma and Louise*, directed by Ridley Scott (1990). What comparative themes do you identify? Are the motor journeys also personal journeys?

— Consider the development of character in the example you have come up with and compare it to Mavis at this point. Is the account of the journey also a version of her personal development?

MAVIS
SECTION 3 (pp. 42–9)

Focus on: mood and tone

ANALYSE AND INTERPRET . . .

— Think about this section of the text as establishing the mood at the Convent. Pick out the words and phrases that set the tone when the community begins to expand with the arrival of Mavis (pp. 42–6). Go on to analyse Mavis's encounter with Mother (pp. 46–8) and the references to the destruction of the Convent with which the novel opens.

DESCRIBE . . .

— Use this analysis to form a description of the novel's mood at this point. Imagine you are writing this for someone unfamiliar with the novel. What elements of the tone do you consider to be most important for your description? Which characters or relationships establish a particular mood?

CONSIDER . . .

— Looking over your description, think about how the mood and tone you have depicted set up expectations for the following sections. For example, how does the tone of Mavis's encounter with Mother establish a connection that you would expect the other women to find special or unusual?

GRACE
SECTION I (pp. 53–62)

Focus on: the theme of desire

DETAIL AND EVALUATE . . .

— In this opening section of 'Grace' the reader is introduced to the characters of KD and Arnette, as well as a third, initially unnamed woman: 'Either the pavement was burning or she had sapphires hidden in her shoes' (p. 53) See pp. 16–17 of the interview for a commentary of this image by Morrison. Paying particular attention to these three characters, detail the different versions of desire with which you are presented here (pp. 53–6).

— Tease out the interrelationships. For example, how does KD's desire for this new woman affect his relationship with Arnette? The ideas may be implicit, so pay careful attention to the more subtle parallels that Morrison makes. For example, look at the juxtaposition of KD's view of the woman with Arnette in the background (pp. 53–4).

ANALYSE . . .

— Now focus your attention on the second part of this section (pp. 56–62). Keeping the theme of desire as your analytical concern, look at the different types of desire that conflict with one another here.

— Break down this analysis by establishing the link between the desire and the character. For instance, KD's desire may be to reject Arnette in favour of his new love interest – how does this conflict with Fleet, or even with Arnette's desires? How do Reverend Misner's desires intrude upon the debate?

— Take the analysis of the conflicting desires that you have identified and think about the different kinds of desire you have examined and how some forms directly oppose others.

GRACE
SECTION 2 (pp. 63–73)

Focus on: the theme of quests

ESTABLISH . . .

'A man and a woman fucking forever' (p. 63). At this point the text focuses on Gigi's quest for two geographical formations: the rocks that resemble a couple perpetually 'fucking', and two trees growing in each other's arms (p. 66).

— The quest narrative is one of the fundamental archetypes of Western tales. Spend just a few minutes as a group thinking about how many you are able to identify quickly. Think about the construction of the quest narrative: what are its basic elements, and what do you need to find in a story in order to name it a 'quest' narrative?

COMPARE . . .

— When you have formulated a working definition of a quest narrative, read closely through this story and identify how this account of Gigi's story fits into your model. What components does it satisfy?

— Also consider the ways in which this account subverts the quest narrative. For example, what gender is the person who traditionally undertakes the quest – and what is their reward? (You might consider quest narratives in films such as *Indiana Jones*, *Sleeping Beauty* or *Shrek*.) What other subversions are there in this story?

— Look over your analysis and consider how the quest narrative is employed here, and how the text manipulates traditional modes of storytelling.

EXTEND . . .

— As you work your way through the novel, you may want

153

to trace other examples of 'quest' narratives and how their manipulation forces the reader to think about the novel's themes in new and surprising ways.

GRACE
SECTION 3 (pp. 73–7)

Focus on: the character of Gigi

IDENTIFY . . .

— Construct a character profile of Gigi from her interaction with KD and Grace. Pay particular attention to the differences between her attitude to Grace as opposed to her lover.

— Look over your analysis and identify which elements of your characterisation you consider to be the most important in terms of understanding Gigi. What frames, or defines, her character?

— Remember to think about other characters' attitudes to her, as well as her perception of herself. Grace and KD also regard her primarily in terms of one defining characteristic.

— Think about her defining characteristic. Is the overt sexuality that Gigi embodies also one of the characterisations of the Convent? If so, who defines it as a primarily sexual location?

Looking over 'Ruby', 'Mavis' and 'Grace'

QUESTIONS FOR DISCUSSION OR ESSAYS

1. Consider the themes of ambiguity and mystery as they are built up in these sections.

2. Analyse either the treatment of mothers or the treatment of brothers in these sections.

3. 'No journey is ever wasted.' Discuss, with reference to *Paradise*.

SENECA
SECTION 1 (pp. 81–8)

Focus on: political history

COMBINE . .
— For a really thorough engagement with history in 'Seneca', combine your work here with your analysis of sections 3 and 4.

RESEARCH . . .
— 'There were no silk stockings in Haven or the world in 1949' (p. 82). 'He'd called Thurgood Marshall a "stir up Negro" for handling the NAACP's segregation suit in Norman' (p. 82). Look at the various specific historical references made here. Choose one reference and investigate its meaning. For example, who are the 'NAACP'? If you are working in a group, assign a topic to each person so that you can pool your research.

REASSESS . . .
— When you have pooled your resources, think about how important the historical context you have formed is to your understanding of this novel.

DISCUSS . . .
— Get together and discuss the implications of your research. How informed were you about the politics of segregation? Did your research extend as far as looking at the history of slavery? If so, how has this affected your attitude to the text? Are you

surprised at how recent the events that you have been researching are? Evaluate the reasons for your answer.

Focus on: language

TEASE OUT . . .

— Analyse the discussion of the Oven (pp. 83–8), focusing on it as an argument about the meaning of words. How is language the topic of the argument here?

— Think about the implications of fighting over language and how it is particularly complex in this instance. For example, is the community fighting over a particular word and its meaning – 'Be versus Beware' (p. 86)? The arguments over language and meaning are the focus of much of 'Seneca' and you may want to extend your analysis beyond p. 88.

SENECA
SECTION 2 (pp. 88–100)

Focus on: the theme of communication

COMPARE AND CONTRAST . . .

— Two perspectives are narrated here: Dovey's and Steward's. Thinking about the theme of communication, examine the couple's explanation of how remote they feel from one another. What are they unable to talk about with one another? Do they offer any explanation for these difficulties, and what do they perceive as being the cause?

CONSIDER . . .

— Having examined the couple's expression of their inability to communicate with one another, look at the other types of communication. For instance, you could focus on Dovey's relationship with her 'Friend' (p. 92). Or you might prefer to look at the theme of communication between the narrator and the reader by examining what the story Steward tells about his father communicates to you as a reader.

SENECA
SECTION 3 (pp. 100–14)

Focus on: personal history

— Amalgamate your work here with your research in section 1 of 'Seneca' for a fuller discussion of history. You could swap the focuses, researching the political references in section 3 and examining the personal references in section 1.

PARALLEL . . .
— Work your way through this section and sketch out the different histories that you are given of Ruby. Look at Soane's version of her son's funeral (pp. 100–7), and then examine Deek's account of the same incident (pp. 111–12). Go on to study his history of Ruby's establishment, the history of the town's formation as a result of his mother's death.

EVALUATE . . .
— Take some time to reflect on how your understanding of Ruby as a town is informed by these personal histories. How does it alter your attitude to the inhabitants of the town? How is your sympathy realigned here?

BRING TOGETHER . . .
— There is a famous feminist phrase: 'The personal is political'. As suggested at the opening of this section, combine your research on the political context of the novel with your

examination of these personal histories. How does your work on each version of history inform the other, as well as your perceptions of the novel?

DISCUSS . . .
In a group, examine the following topics for discussion:

- The idea of context: how important are histories to your textual understanding?
- How important is the political history you have researched in forming your attitude to the community at Ruby?
- Are personal histories essential in creating empathy? Without a personal account, is political history simply theory that the reader can ignore?
- Do you need both the personal and the political to create a historical context?

SENECA
SECTION 4 (pp. 115–24)

Focus on: narrative structure

CHARACTERISE AND IDENTIFY . . .
— Examine closely the plot and tone of this section of narratives. Which characters does it centre upon, and what occurs? How would you characterise the mood of this section? (You may want to sub-divide the section so that you can identify mood shifts.)

COMPARE . . .
— When you have worked through the structure of the section, think about its place in 'Seneca' – how is it juxtaposed with the previous focus on Dovey, Steward, Deek and Soane?

Are different characters focusing on the same themes and issues? Are they linked, as well as separated, by narrative shifts?

— Is the tone consistent with the previous section? If not, how is it different? Does it create a sense of relief because the mood is lighter? Or is there in fact a sense of foreboding through a continuously dark mood? (You may want to argue the case for both!)

— By analysing this section in relation to what comes before and after it, concentrate your thoughts on narrative structure and think about how 'Seneca's' narrative structure privileges certain themes and characters.

SENECA
SECTION 5 (pp. 124–30)

Focus on: the theme of abandonment

RELATE AND EVALUATE . . .

— In this section two women's tales are closely combined. Look at the narrative strands of each and think about the links between them. Start with the paralleled actions of both, and then pick out the metaphors and phrases that link them. How are the two conceptually linked for the reader?

— Having identified the language and plot links, think about thematic connections. How are the two women tied to one another through the theme of abandonment? How, for example, is Sweetie presented as being simultaneously abandoned and abandoning?

EXPLORE . . .

— Think about how the thematic and linguistic ties between the women create certain expectations in you, as a reader. What do you expect to happen to the two women? How does the narrative, through your expectations, establish a connection with the Convent through the theme of abandonment?

SENECA
SECTION 6 (pp. 130–8)

Focus on: the theme of absence

READ CLOSELY AND SEARCH . . .

> 'You have to help me,' she said. 'You have to. I've
> been raped and it's almost August.'
>   Only part of that was true. (p. 77)

— This is the last sentence from 'Grace'; it is centred on an ambiguity, or absence, as the reader is not told which of the statements is true. Work your way closely through Seneca's narration of her life before arriving at the Convent. However, instead of focusing on the details you are given, read this section looking at what you are *not* told. What is absent from Seneca's narration?

DEVELOP . . .

— Reading over the textual absences you have noted, get into pairs and develop your ideas about how what you do *not* know affects your understanding of Seneca. What assumptions have you had to make in order to make sense of her as a character? Which pieces of information are you particularly looking to discover?

INCORPORATE . . .

— Take this focus on the absent and develop your ideas in relation to section 5 and your discussion of abandonment. How is the idea of absent information linked to the absences of Seneca's childhood?

REFLECT . . .
— Think about the importance of absence in constructing a story. Choosing what to leave out of a tale is as fundamental as deciding what to include, so reflect upon how the absences you have identified here have affected your understanding of this section of the novel. (You may want to extend your analysis to include other parts of the text, or to return to this topic when you have worked your way through the novel as a whole.)

Looking over 'Seneca'

QUESTIONS FOR DISCUSSION OR ESSAYS
1. Consider the themes of absence and abandonment here.

2. 'Without language, there can be no history.' Discuss, with reference to *Paradise*.

3. Explain and assess the presentation of Seneca's character.

DIVINE
SECTION 1 (pp. 141–55)

Focus on: perspectives

DISTINGUISH . . .
— 'Divine' opens with the marriage of KD and Arnette. Work your way through this section and demarcate the various speakers and narrators. How many different voices do you encounter in this section?

ASSESS . . .

— Examine the different voices, focusing on their perspective on KD and Arnette's marriage. How many of the characters whose perspective you are given are actually thinking or talking about the wedding itself?

— Assess Morrison's employment of multiple perspectives here. Use the following questions as a means of tackling the issue:

- What impact do you regard the different voices as having upon the reader?
- How does this influence your attitude to the wedding?
- Does the wedding itself remain the focus of the community with which you are presented here?

Focus on: the theme of religion

COMPARE AND CONTRAST . . .

— Examine the wedding service as given by Pulliam and Misner (pp. 141–2, 144–7). What contrasts these religious men? How is Pulliam's sermon different from Misner's? Bear in mind the following issues as you analyse the differences between the two 'sermons':

- Speech: do the men speak directly to the congregation/the reader? Do they, in fact, speak at all?
- Gesture: what other means do the men use to communicate their religious statement?
- Theme: what differences do you identify in the men's religious positions? How do they oppose one another directly or indirectly? What religious values do the men espouse? How are these values represented in their speech and actions at the wedding?
- Structure: how is this part of the narrative constructed to

set the two men up in opposition to one another? Where is the reader located in this debate? Think about the opening sentence, 'Let me tell you about love' (p. 141). Is the reader part of the congregation here? What differences does it make to your consideration of religion at this point to be included in the religious community?

DIVINE
SECTION 2 (pp. 155–62)

Focus on: the theme of community

ANALYSE . . .
— After the marriage ceremony, the congregation attends the celebration of the wedding at Deek's house, to which the Convent women have been invited. Looking at this passage, think about how the women facilitate the re-creation of the community of Ruby. What cracks are apparent in the community before the women arrive, and how does their attendance at the party help to recement it?

EXTEND . . .
— Get together in a group and discuss the idea of community – how is a community formed? Think about yourself: what communities do you consider yourself to be a member of? What qualities make you a member of that particular community?
— While discussing the idea of a community, think about this passage and the idea of inclusion and exclusion. You have considered what you share with other members of the communities you have identified, but think also about how that automatically excludes some people from membership. How important is this exclusion in defining what makes up a community? (You might

like to discuss examples such as asylum and becoming part of a national community; or, if some communities seem straightforward – for example, based on gender – which community does a transsexual belong to?)

DIVINE
SECTION 3 (pp. 162–72)

Focus on: ambiguity

REVISE AND REFRESH . . .

— At the outset of the novel you were asked to focus your critique on the notion of ambiguity. Return to your discussion of it and remind yourself of the work you did on the concept. For example, how did Morrison foreground ambiguity in this novel?

REASSESS AND RELATE . . .

— Turn your attention to the incidents that take place in this section (pp. 162–9). What occurs on the journey back from Ruby? What kind of explanation are you given for the fight between the two women? How does the detailed explanation of the build-up to the argument (pp. 162–8) and its aftermath (pp. 169–72) normalise the incident for the reader? How do we, as readers, make sense of what occurs through the information we are given?

— Now focus your attention on the short paragraph on p. 169 which gives an account of a 'trucker'. Here Morrison plays with perspective to establish a profound insecurity in the trucker. What does he think is going on as he drives past?

— Think about the shift between the detailed explanation that the reader is given as opposed to the brief encounter with the trucker. How does the trucker's misconception highlight the theme of ambiguity?

TRANSFORM . . .

— Take the events of this section and rewrite them from the perspective of the trucker. How do the events themselves change as he attempts to make sense of what he witnesses?

RECONSIDER . . .

— Taking what you have learned from the analysis and creative exercise, think about this question, which was put to you at the start of your analysis of *Paradise*: what is the relationship between the text's ambiguities and the theme of judgement in the novel?

DIVINE
SECTION 4 (pp. 172–82)

Focus on: naming

DISCOVER AND INTERPRET . . .

— 'She turned to Pallas. "They like you too. They think you're divine"' (p. 182). This final part of 'Divine' tells the story of Pallas's arrival at the Convent. In fact, much of the section is devoted to Pallas. Before considering the complex relationship of naming in *Paradise*, discover what you can about the names of the characters in this section.

— For example, Pallas is a Roman goddess – so discover what she represents. What does Seneca mean? What is signified by the name 'Divine'?

— When you have researched the names' meanings think about the decision to entitle Pallas's section 'Divine'. What does Gigi mean by naming her through the presence of ghosts?

EXTEND . . .

— As you come across new names, extend your analysis to incorporate characters in other sections of the novel, such as Consolata.

— Also extend your analysis to consider naming in a broader context. Think about the title of the novel itself and its relation to naming. Adam and Eve were given, by God, the animals. Think about how names frame identity here and how Morrison plays upon them. (You could incorporate the naming of the town in your analysis, or even extend it to consider the trilogy as a whole, incorporating Joe Trace in *Jazz* or Belóved in *Beloved*.)

Looking over 'Divine'

QUESTIONS FOR DISCUSSION OR ESSAYS

1. Analyse the use of perspectives and point of view in the novel so far.

2. How does Morrison create a sense of place and period in *Paradise*?

3. 'Naming is power.' Discuss, with reference to *Paradise*.

4. 'The ghosts of *Beloved* and *Jazz* haunt the world of *Paradise*.' Discuss.

PATRICIA
SECTION 1 (pp. 185–93)

Focus on: the theme of trees

EXAMINE . . .

— The opening of Patricia's section starts with the line 'Bells and pine trees, cut from green and red construction paper'. Examine the symbolic use of trees in this section. What are they taken to represent, and how are they used by Patricia and the community she is a part of?

TRACE AND DETERMINE . . .

— Focus particularly on the employment of the idea of the 'family tree'. You might choose to trace the interlinked families that Patricia describes and to map out the family tree she talks about. Or you may prefer to annotate your notes on individual characters with the information that Patricia gives you here.

— Think about how her sketching out of characters' blood-links enlightens your understanding of the community.

EVALUATE . . .

— Drawing on your consideration of Patricia's family tree, evaluate her attitude to the history that she is constructing:

- How does she regard the family tree she has produced?
- Think particularly about her suggestion that it complicates rather than simplifies relationships (pp. 187–9).
- How does her family tree 'grow' from the original 'genealogy' (p. 187)?

RE-EVALUATE

— Relate your discussion of family trees to other thematic concerns you have focused on. You might like to think about Patricia's family tree and her narration of its contents in relation to your analysis of personal and public histories (sections 1 and 3 of 'Divine'). Or you might wish to extend your analysis still further to think about the symbolism of trees in either *Beloved* or *Jazz*. How are trees employed in either text (think about the Clearing in *Beloved*, or Sethe's scar, or about Joe and Violet's account of the countryside in *Jazz*)?

PATRICIA
SECTION 2 (pp. 193–204)

Focus on: 'eight-rock'

INTERROGATE AND DISCUSS . . .

— Patricia provides you with a definition of what it means to be 'eight-rock' (p. 193). Look closely at her definition, thinking about the employment of a geographical metaphor here. Then extend your analysis to cover her assessment of what this conception of racial purity has meant for the community of Ruby.

— Get into groups and discuss the idea of a pure blood-line. Think about its connection to the extreme right wing and Fascism.

— Ask yourselves the following questions as you examine this means of differentiation within the community:

- How does the story of the nativity, and the children involved, highlight the problems of such a position?
- Do you regard it as a gesture of empowerment, a reclamation of beauty other than on grounds of whiteness?
- How does Patricia's relationship to Billy Delia embody the difficulties of the community's espousal of the importance of 'eight-rock'?

ANALYSE AND RELATE . . .

— Think about the political consequences of your discussion and about Morrison's decision to personalise the debate through the character of Patricia. How is she used as a literary and narrative device in order to suggest a particular set of ideas to the reader? (You may want to tie your discussion in to your understanding of the history of slavery, particularly if you have studied *Beloved*.)

PATRICIA
SECTION 3 (pp. 204–10)

Focus on: the 1960s and 1970s

DEVELOP . . .

— *Paradise* is a closely contextualised novel. There are frequent references to what is happening in the United States at the point in place and time in which the novel is set. Work together and develop the political historical research that you undertook as part of the first section in 'Seneca' to fill out your knowledge of the period.

— For example, who are the 'panthers' (p. 207)? Who is Malcolm X? Discover more about the debate that Reverend Misner and Patricia have about the idea that the black community's home is in 'Africa' (p. 210).

LOCATE AND IMMERSE . . .

— As well as developing your understanding of the politics surrounding the characters' discussion, try and discover more about the cultural clash between the generations that they discuss.

— Start with the three topics below and investigate 1960s' and 1970s' black culture and its iconic status. Again, pool your group's knowledge:

- Who were black cultural icons of the 1960s and 1970s such as Ali and X?
- What is blaxsploitation?
- Who were the stars of Motown?

— Take the opportunity through your research to listen to and watch the music and films you are identifying. Think about how access to cultural references gives an insight into a particular period.

PATRICIA
SECTION 4 (pp. 211–17)

Focus on: the theme of identity

EXAMINE AND DETAIL . . .

— Towards the end of the section devoted to Pat, both she and Misner reflect upon how they regard the community of Ruby to be 'doomed'. First, examine Misner's account of the fate he predicts for them (pp. 211–13).

— Second, look at Patricia's thoughts on her relationship with Misner, her family and the community at large (pp. 213–17).

— Work closely through the text and select the phrases – literal, metaphoric and symbolic – which suggest her version of the crisis of identity that Ruby faces. Be specific about the language that conveys the sense of a collapse in the community's ideals.

CONSIDER AND LINK . . .

— Think about Morrison's construction of this section of 'Patricia'. Analyse the means by which she conveys a crisis in terms of black identity, by improving your knowledge of the context of the novel and through close linguistic analysis.

— Think about the construction of the sections. How does the focus on the town in Patricia's section contrast with the focus on events at the Convent in 'Divine' and what is coming up in 'Consolata'? This section particularly investigates the politics of identity. How is that complicated by not knowing which woman at the Convent is white?

— Now link your analysis to the thematic implications for the novel as a whole. Think about how this crisis of identity is suggested in the novel's title. Just as Adam and Eve are expelled from Eden, does the title of the novel suggest an inevitable collapse for the community of Ruby? Come back to this question as you continue your progress through the novel.

CONSOLATA
SECTION 1 (pp. 221–30)

Focus on: the character of Consolata

SKETCH . . .

— Map out a brief character analysis of Connie from the descriptions you are given here. Do you understand her as a result of this account of her childhood? What facets of her character are you particularly aware of here?

DETAIL AND ANALYSE . . .

— The opening section of 'Consolata' gives the reader a framing narrative for the character. It begins: 'In the good clean darkness of the cellar, Consolata woke to the wrenching disappointment of not having died the night before' (p. 221). Analyse the structure of this section, looking at the order in which information about Connie is given. How does opening with her death influence our understanding of her character?

— Then work your way through the section picking out the details that suggest Connie's character. Think particularly about *how* they are presented to you.

COMBINE . . .

— When you have looked at the structure of the narrative, combine your structural analysis with your characterisation of Connie. Think about how she is distinguished for the reader from the rest of the women at the Convent. Look both at how she herself characterises her alienation and at how the structure of this section sets her apart from the others. You may want to discover what 'Consolata' means, and incorporate this into your structural and thematic analysis.

CONSOLATA
SECTION 2 (pp. 230–5)

Focus on: the theme of the Bible

DISCOVER AND READ . . .

— Look at the story of Esau and Jacob in Genesis (chapters 27–9), and of Cain and Abel (chapter 3), and think about parallels between the two pairs of brothers and Deek and Steward. Pick out the specific narrative and plot details that are reflected in all three narratives. How, for example, is the brothers' jealousy over women mirrored by the parables?

EXPLORE . . .

— Think about the text's relationship to the Bible. How does your attitude to the text change when you consider its use of parables? (You may want to take examples from elsewhere in the novel.) How is your attitude affected by your knowledge of Christian doctrine? For example, how does your understanding of Genesis and Eden set up certain expectations for the text?

RETURN AND APPLY . . .

— Refocus your attention on the excerpt. How does your understanding of the biblical precedents depersonalise the characters? Does it transfer them to the level of icons? If so, how does this alter your reading of the brothers?

CONSOLATA
SECTION 3 (pp. 235–48)

Focus on: the theme of sin

LIST . . .

— This section details both the collapse of Consolata's relationship with Deek and her blossoming friendship with Soane, his wife. List the references to sin in this section. In how many different ways are ideas about what is 'sinful' suggested?

— As well as the behaviour of specific characters, think about overall themes such as the context of the section. For example, how does the Convent frame the affair in terms of sin?

DEFINE . . .

— Look over your list and work together, in pairs or larger groups, to construct a definition of 'sin'. How do you understand it? Does it only have meaning in a particular religious context such as Catholicism? Is it meaningful to those who do not characterise themselves as Christian? What is an atheist definition of 'sin', or is the word redundant to atheists?

APPLY . . .

— Look over your list of 'sins' and think about how they are complicated by your definition. Focus particularly on the clash of religious practices that takes place at the end of this section (pp. 242–8). How does the idea of 'sin' complicate life for Consolata, for instance?

Focus on: the theme of friendship

INTERPRET . . .

— 'Consolata rose from her chair as if summoned by the sheriff or an angel. In a way it was both, in the shape of a young woman, exhausted, breathing hard but ramrod straight'

173

(p. 238). By focusing on the friendship of Soane and Consolata, think about the discussion of friendship in this section. How do trials and difficulties cement their friendship?

DISCUSS . . .

— In groups, talk about the blueprint for friendship with which you are presented here. Why is the friendship so surprising? How do the women describe their closeness to one another here? Who narrates their friendship – is it in fact either of the women, or a third voice?

— Think about unlikely friendships that you are aware of – they may be personal experiences or fictional examples that you are familiar with. How do common obstacles help to form friendships? What role does respect play in a friendship like Soane and Consolata's? Do you believe it to be a genuine friendship, or are you suspicious of it?

— Come back to these questions at the end of the novel, thinking about the quality of loyalty displayed between the two women.

LINK . . .

— Tie in this discussion of friendship with your analysis of the treatment of 'sin' here. How does the motivation of friendship alter your attitude to the 'sinful'? Does something become less sinful when it is motivated by friendship? (You may want to compare and contrast the discussion of friends here with your analysis of the brothers in section 3 of 'Ruby', or in section 2 of 'Consolata'.)

CONSOLATA
SECTION 4 (pp. 248–52)

Focus on: cycles

ANALYSE AND REFLECT . . .

— Tease out the interweaving stories narrated here. Look both at the account of Pallas and the 'girl from Ruby' (p. 249) and at the man who returns to visit Connie (pp. 251–2). Analyse how the four narratives are told by paralleling each other here. For example, you learn about Pallas indirectly through Connie's account of another young woman.

— How do the parallel tales affect you as a reader? Think about how cycles, or patterns, are established. How are expectations created for the future through the linking of past stories to one another?

INTERPRET . . .

— Think about story cycles. Often we expect a story to have a beginning, middle and end. How is this pattern complicated by the idea of the cycle: stories linking together or repeating themselves?

— Sometimes cyclical stories are gendered as being 'female' as opposed to linear 'male' narratives. Extend your analysis to think about the other storytelling cycles you encounter here – what other patterns of telling do you get? How often is the same story retold?

— How do you interpret these cycles in terms of Morrison's novel? Is it a 'female' narrative? Or would you want to distinguish between different elements of the novel, entitling the Convent narratives as 'female' as opposed to other 'male' narratives? (Cite closely the textual evidence that supports your argument.)

CONSOLATA
SECTION 5 (pp. 252–62)

Focus on: language and tone

EXTRACT AND ANALYSE . . .

— Throughout this passage details of the preparation of a meal are intercut. Extract the paragraphs that focus on the meal and place them side-by-side, then think about this as a single 'story'.

— Look closely at the details of preparation and cooking that you are given. What particularly strikes you about the description?

EXAMINE . . .

— Now think about why Morrison decides to divide this narrative into stages. What happens when you regard the story in its component parts, rather than combined in the single story that you have described above?

— Why do you think Morrison juxtaposes the meal's preparation with other narratives? How does the extended account link the passages that it surrounds?

— Look at the specific language of the meal preparation and think about how the metaphors and phrases inform your interpretation of the other passages.

— How is the meal used to set a certain mood or tone here? Is it mirroring natural life, for example, suggesting the time that the preparation takes? Or are the women like the food — are they objects that Connie prepares for life, just as she creates the meal?

Focus on: personal history

REFRESH . . .

— At the opening of the novel you may have studied the

contrasting personal histories of the inhabitants of Ruby. Look over your notes at this point to remind yourself of your consideration of personal histories and how they determine your attitude to certain characters. (If you did not attempt this exercise, look back at the issues highlighted to give you an idea of what is meant here by personal history.)

COMPARE AND CONTRAST . . .

— Having reminded yourself of the notion of personal histories, explore the various accounts that you are given here of the women at the Convent. Think about their different versions of leaving and returning to the Convent.

— Focus first on what links the narratives. Think about which concerns they all seem to have. Are there themes that connect them? Are they linked through their affection for Connie?

— Then turn your attention to what contrasts the women. For example, look at Gigi's plan to escape, as contrasted with Mavis's desire to return to the Convent when she remembers being away from it.

EXPLORE . . .

— Bring together your analysis of the separate accounts. Do these personal histories give you an insight into each character, or do you read them rather as the history of the Convent?

— Explore the idea of personal history here – do these accounts remain separate? Do you react to them as partial accounts that link to give you greater insight into a larger context – that of the Convent?

— Perhaps in your analysis you identified a particular theme that links the women. Does your interest in a particular theme influence your overall attitude?

COMBINE . . .

— Integrate your analysis of the mood and tone of this section with the question of personal histories. Bring in your discussion of the preparation of the meal. Does it link the stories – changing them from personal histories to one stream of thought, or *stream of consciousness* – as Connie cooks? How are the personal histories combined like ingredients in the meal?

CONSOLATA
SECTION 6 (pp. 262–6)

Focus on: art

RESEARCH AND INTERROGATE . . .
— Debate the idea of 'art' – what is art? You may want to inform your discussion through references to contemporary debates about art. Discover what the Turner Prize is, for example. How has it fuelled debates about art? Bear in mind issues such as:

- Expression: is art about self-expression? Expressing a society's views? A government's ideas? A nation's perspective?
- Value: does art have to be expensive?
- Form: how many different types of art do you recognise? Is graffiti art?

ANALYSE . . .
— When you have examined what you understand to be 'art', return your attention to the novel. Do the women's drawings fit your conception of 'art'? If not, why not?
— Paying close attention to the passage, think about the women's attitude to their drawings – do they regard them as art?
— When you have reached a conclusion, think about how

valuable their perspective is – if an 'artist' tells you it is 'art', would you challenge them? Would you characterise these women as artists?

RETURN . . .

—— Come back to this question when you have completed your analysis. How does the attitude to the drawings of the people of Ruby inform your understanding? (Be careful about distinguishing between the narrator's position and that of the characters.) Is art, by definition, incomprehensible to some?

Looking over 'Patricia' and 'Consolata'

QUESTIONS FOR DISCUSSION OR ESSAYS

1.   Consider the ways in which Morrison uses the idea of the tree and the 'family tree' in this novel, or in the trilogy as a whole.

2.   Look up the derivations of Patricia's and Consolata's names. How does the etymology of their names connect to their characterisation and actions in the novel?

3.   Why is food, and the preparation of food, a key theme in this novel?

4.   Analyse the theme of blood and blood-lines in the novel so far.

LONE
SECTION I (pp. 269–80)

Focus on: the theme of isolation and exclusion

CONCEPTUALISE . . .

— Think about this opening section and its name, 'Lone'. Rather than performing a character analysis, think about what it means to be 'lone'. How is it different from being 'alone', for example? What is a 'loner'?

— Work through the passage, thinking not only about the character of 'Lone', but also about the other characters discussed here. How are they isolated from one another – physically, emotionally, psychologically?

DEVELOP . . .

— Extend your analysis of isolation and the idea of a loner to think about isolation through exclusion. For instance, take Lone's observations about the men attacking the Convent: 'So, Lone thought, the fangs and the tail are somewhere else' (p. 276). The women are isolated by choice, according to Lone, but they are punished for this separation. Here it is in fact the community of Ruby that is excluded, while it appears that it is the Convent.

COMPARE . . .

— Re-examine this opening, thinking about the complex relationship of isolation to exclusion. You may want to focus on the allusion in the above quotation to Satan and Paradise. Compare the interrelations of exclusion and isolation in Genesis to the patterns that you observe in *Paradise*. Look both at Satan's exclusion as a fallen angel and at the fall from grace of Adam and Eve.

— Either orally or in written form, construct your analysis of this debate around the following statement: Lone is named after isolation, but she embodies the spirit of the community; instead, the community that she attempts to relate to embodies isolation and exclusion.

Focus on: pace

TRACE AND EVALUATE . . .

— Work in pairs to distinguish and evaluate the mechanisms by which Morrison increases the pace at this point in the narrative. How does she suggest a sense of urgency for the crisis that is looming?

— Be specific in your analysis, looking at the language and structure of this passage. Think in detail about the mechanics of the increase in pace that you identify.

— Look at the interrelation of characters, the shifts of setting, the use of physical journeys to mirror less literal movements.

EXTEND . . .

— When you have selected phrases that support your position, think about how the idea of prevention is used to accelerate the pace. Expand your discussion to include the rest of the novel. How, for example, do Lone's actions contrast with the opening of the novel?

— How does your knowledge of the outcome affect the pace at this point? Is pace hard to create because we already know the result, or does this somehow increase our desire for prevention, and thus create pace?

LONE
SECTION 2 (pp. 280–92)

Focus on: denouement

DISCOVER . . .

— Use the glossary provided, and additional research, to find out what the word *denouement* means.

TEST . . .

— 'Lone sighs. "Well, the dead don't move . . . No bodies. Nothing. Even the Cadillac was gone."' To what extent does the word 'denouement' cover this section of the novel? Is it suitably described as the novel's denouement? If not, in what ways does it fail to fit your definition? What expectations do you have of a denouement, and how does this section of text fail to meet them?
— Work closely through the passage, looking at how narratives are piled on top of one another. Think also about the details of the crisis that are given here. (You may want to compare this section to the opening account of the men's arrival at the Convent.)

REVISE . . .

— Consider the surprises you encounter here. How does this section work in terms of satisfying your curiosity about the events at the Convent? (Look over your analysis of ambiguity in section 1 of 'Ruby'.) Think particularly about how ambiguities are maintained here.

SCAN . . .

— Taking account of the text as a whole, is there any other section of narrative that satisfies your definition (p. 295, opening paragraph, for example)? Be clear about your criteria and how well any part of the text meets them.

— When you have considered this question, think more closely about the relationship to ambiguity in the novel. How is the denouement complicated by Morrison's refusal to clarify some of the novel's central ambiguities?

SAVE-MARIE
SECTION 1 (pp. 295–303)

Focus on: the theme of forgiveness

ANALYSE AND EXPLORE . . .
— Take one of the three examples of forgiveness from this section given below and explore the novel's treatment of it. Before conducting your analysis, think about how you under-stand the term:

● What is forgiveness as a Christian term?
● Is it permanent?
● Whose is it to give?

1. The burial of Sweetie's child. How is the creation of the cemetery presented as a *paradigm* of the changes that have taken place in Ruby? What is she refusing to forgive?

2. Lone's breakdown. How does it suggest a lack of forgive-ness on the part of others towards her? How does she inter-pret the actions of the community?

3. The suggestion, at the point at which Connie is shot, is that Deek does not want her murdered, despite his active role in the pursuit of the women at the Convent. Think care-fully about forgiveness as Reverend Misner and Deek dis-cuss it (pp. 299–303). How does their conversation suggest

both a change in Deek's character and the complexity of forgiveness in this novel? Does he forgive Steward? (You may
want to jot down other incidences of characters forgiving,
or refusing to forgive, one another — such as Soane and
Connie.)

SAVE-MARIE
SECTION 2 (pp. 303–17)

Focus on: structure — happy endings

INTERROGATE . . .
— Read through the tales that tie up the novel, selecting the
ways in which they are framed as happy endings. How are they
structured in order to suggest resolution for individual characters (Mavis, Gigi, Pallas and Seneca)? How are they satisfying? How do they reflect what you, as a reader, would like
for the characters in question?

NOTE . . .
— Then reread the section, noting down every time you, as
a reader, have to assume knowledge in order to make sense of
these sections.

REFLECT . . .
— Use your list to think about the nature of the happy ending.
How are we, as readers, encouraged to look for a happy ending?
How prepared are we to do the work to engineer one when it
isn't clearly presented?

Focus: on ambiguity

EXAMINE . . .

— Use your discussion of the nature of a happy ending to think about the ambiguities that Morrison refuses to clarify at this point. Are any of the characters directly named here, for example?

— Earlier in 'Save-Marie' the reader is told that multiple fracturing versions of what happened to the women are circulating. Do you believe these accounts? In what ways does the central ambiguity around which the text revolves stop us reacting too simplistically to these narratives?

— What role does our desire for resolution play here? Are we, as readers, determined to save the characters?

REFLECT . . .

— Think about the ambiguity of the title of the section in relation to these stories. We are told that the child was named as a form of protection, but we only encounter her at her burial. Think about the Christian associations of being 'saved' and about the name 'Marie'.

— Also look at the linguistic ambiguity – for example, the relation of 'Save-Marie' to 'Save Me'. Who is 'me'? Is this a reference to the reader?

SAVE-MARIE
SECTION 3 (p. 318)

Focus on: Paradise

INVESTIGATE . . .

— Look closely at this final page and think about the myth of Paradise. Use the resources provided on pp. 190–2, or get help from your group leader or teacher, to ensure that you understand this passage fully. For example, who is 'Piedade' (p. 318)? What is 'cerulean' (p. 318)?

DISCUSS . . .

— When you have established that you understand the language used here, get together and talk about what you understand by 'Paradise' at this point. You could compare it to other versions, such as the Bible's in Genesis, John Milton's *Paradise Lost* (1667) or *Utopia* (1516) by Thomas More.

— Talk about these divergent versions of Paradise. What strikes you particularly about this framing paragraph? How would you characterise Morrison's version of Paradise here?

BIND . . .

— Combine your varying analyses to think about the relationship of the title to the substance of the text. What versions of Paradise are you presented with here? How do they conflict with one another?

— What kind of resolution is suggested in this final vision?

Looking over 'Lone' and 'Save-Marie'

QUESTIONS FOR DISCUSSION OR ESSAYS

1. Why forgive? Discuss with reference to *Paradise*.

2. Contrast the themes of solitude and community in this section of the novel.

3. What concepts of 'Paradise' are offered in Morrison's *Paradise*?

Looking back over the whole novel

QUESTIONS FOR DISCUSSION OR ESSAYS

1. Analyse the theme of journeying and journeys in *Paradise* and in the trilogy as a whole.

2. 'The written word can always be revised. The spoken word can never be retracted.' Consider the presentation of literacy and orality in Morrison's novels and assess their relative values.

3. 'Improvisation is Morrison's method.' Discuss.

4. Discuss the theme of gender in *Paradise*.

5. Consider how faith is presented in *Paradise*.

6. Examine notions of isolation and community in the novel.

7. Discuss the theme of abandonment in *Paradise*.

8. Consider how personal and political narratives are related in *Paradise*.

Contexts, comparisons and complementary readings

PARADISE

Paradise is the final novel in the trilogy, and as such many of the contexts suggested below revisit and expand upon material covered in the detailed readings of the two preceding novels or in the analysis of *Paradise* itself. If you have looked at the more contextual exercises already suggested, then use them as a springboard for this fuller discussion. If you didn't look at those facets of the novel, then this section provides an opportunity to explore other aspects of the novel.

These sections suggest contextual and comparative ways of reading these three novels by Morrison. You can put your reading in a social, historical or literary context. You can make comparisons – again, social, literary or historical – with other texts. Or you can choose complementary works (of whatever kind) – that is, works of art, literary works, social reportage or facts that illuminate the text, by giving a framework to references that you currently find oblique. Some of the suggested contexts are directly connected to the books, in that they give you precise literary or social frames within which to situate the novel. In turn, these are either related to the period within which the novel is set, or to the time – now – when you are reading it.

Some of these examples are designed to suggest books or other texts that may make useful sources for comparison (or for complementary purposes) when you are reading *Paradise*. They may be related to literary or critical themes, or they may be relevant to social and cultural themes current 'then' or 'now'.

Your contextual research on this text will prove extremely useful in your work on the other books in the trilogy. For example, here your research encourages a consideration of man versus woman, which reappears with a slightly different focus in both *Beloved* and *Jazz*, where the focus is on the maternal, although these contexts could be fruitfully combined. Bring these discussions together to give you an overall response to the trilogy.

Focus on: Paradise

RESEARCH AND CONSIDER . . .

— All three texts in the trilogy are closely related to specific biblical texts. In your detailed analysis, numerous biblical parallels were suggested for the narrative. Obtain a copy of the Old Testament and read the Book of Genesis. Draw on the parallels with *Paradise* to perform a thorough analysis of the relationship between the two texts.

— In your reading of Genesis pay particular attention to:

- The description of sin and its complexity. From your reading, how do you understand the phrase 'Original sin'?
- The idea of knowledge. What role does it play in the original fall from grace of Adam and Eve?

— In contemporary society we tend to prize knowledge and

reward those who seek it. How is this at odds with the idea of Eve and the apple? Think about this understanding of knowledge and how alien it is to us as a concept.

— Then explore how 'Original sin' extends from the fall of Adam and Eve through the lineages that are traced. Concentrate on division — how are families continually split here through jealousy and desire? Also look at the association of knowledge with trickery, suspicion and the failure to trust in God. How is the idea of knowledge associated here with what we might regard as 'negative' qualities?

— Use the following questions to focus your analysis in terms of *Paradise* and its relationship with Genesis:

● How many different versions of Eden are you presented with in this novel? (Remember to consider the different versions of the afterlife of the women of the Convent that you are presented with, as well as the Ruby Convent opposition.) How does Satan, or the serpent, occur in the novel?

● How are the brothers Deacon and Steward paralleled by either Cain and Abel or Esau and Jacob (see the exercises on p. 173)?

● How do the arguments over the Oven work as a paradigm for the apple? How is knowledge here seen as demystifying and alienating, paralleling Adam and Eve's expulsion from Paradise?

HISTORICISE AND DEVELOP . . .

— The history of the notion of Paradise is long and complex, but certain examples remain central in terms of its literary treatment. Look at both John Milton's *Paradise Lost* (1667) and Thomas More's *Utopia* (1516) and trace the development of the idea of 'Original sin'.

— How do these influential writers understand the idea of 'Original sin'? What is their version of knowledge? Do they regard it as the antithesis of faith? (Think about the idea of proving God empirically in order to clarify your thoughts.)

LINK . . .
— Combine your literary and historical research in order to re-interpret Morrison's complication of 'Paradise' in this novel. How does your analysis alter or develop your understanding?
— Return to the exercises on the idea of Paradise – focus on the Oven and its debate about knowledge and 'reading', or interpretation. Also think about the idea of expulsion as the collapse of Haven is mentioned throughout the narrative.

Focus on: man versus woman

ESTABLISH AND CATEGORISE . . .
— Divisions along lines of gender are clearly demarcated in this novel. Draw up a framework that categorises what you consider to be 'female' as opposed to 'male' in this text. For example, is aggression 'male'? When you have drawn up your list of characteristics, extend them by thinking about how you would separate ideas of desire. What makes a man desirable, as opposed to a woman?
— Look at the list below: does it ring true for you in terms of common conceptions?

Men	Women
Feeling	Intelligence
Gracefulness	Earning power
Blonde	Physical force

TALK OVER . . .
— Now question *why* you might regard this list as incorrect.

Think about the extent to which women are regarded in terms of an object – focusing on their beauty or physical attributes. Men are often regarded as being scopophilic, which means that they are drawn predominantly by images or visual stimulus. (Thus the argument runs that pornography appeals to men more than women because men like to look.)

— In the novel, Gigi's physical presence is what interests both KD and Grace. Think about how she does or does not fit the categorisations you have observed.

DISCOVER AND COMBINE . . .

— Biblical allusions in the text have been highlighted in terms of the Old Testament, but now a New Testament concern becomes particularly relevant. The binary opposition of the Virgin/Whore is directly traceable to biblical imagery. Research about the Virgin Mary and Mary Magdalene, and compare the contrasting notions of femininity that they represent.

— How do these iconic female identities inform and complicate *Paradise*? Think about how they are collapsed in the character of Consolata.

LIST AND EVALUATE . . .

— When you have thought about the textual relationship here, go on to consider how these formations still inform our lives today. List all the words you can think of which are used to insult women. In assessing your list, think about how many of them relate to sexuality and the idea of the 'whore'. How are women still caught up in definitions that place them diametrically in one camp or the other? How is the binary opposition sustained?

EXPLORE . . .

— There is a set of chapters of the Bible known as the Apocrypha. Discover what this means and then identify the story of Lilith. It offers an alternative narrative to the Adam and Eve tale, as Lilith precedes Eve as the first woman in Eden. Think about how this narrative is potentially empowering. How does it disrupt the association of women with sin, which through the Virgin/Whore binary comes to inextricably bind sin and sexuality?

Focus on: *the theme of creativity*

RESEARCH AND COMPARE . . .

— Read Alice Walker's essay 'In Search of Our Mothers' Gardens' (1983). It is a homage to the writer's own mother and her brave determination to nurture her capacity for love and creativity in the face of abject poverty. But it is also a politicised call to women to express themselves and respect their sense of identity and worth. How does Walker's political and personal project compare with that delineated by Morrison in *Paradise*, and in the trilogy as a whole?

Reference

Critical Overview

When examining critical work on Morrison the best place to begin is with the author herself. Morrison worked for years as an editor before she launched her writing career, and now lectures at Princeton University, USA. She is an unusual writer, being both a critic and an author. Her critical work entitled *Playing in the Dark, Whiteness and the Literary Imagination*, tackles constructions of colour and racial distinction in works of fiction. This may be useful in your analysis of her treatment of colour, particularly in *Paradise*. You may also find her essay in a collection *The House That Race Built*, edited by Wahneema Lubiano, useful, as it provides a context for thinking about how racist attitudes are produced. Perhaps her most famous discussion, in that it garnered a great deal of press attention, is *Birth of a Nation 'hood: Gaze, Script and Spectacle in the O. J. Simpson Case* in which Morrison tackles O. J. Simpson's treatment as 'criminal'. She examines the consequences of racial stereotyping for his case.

However, whilst Morrison's own critical work is both useful in terms of your analysis of her novels, and provides an excellent example of first-rate writing, it is important to remember that even in relation to her own novels she is just another critical voice. She is not given special authority regarding her texts, and, as a critic, you can take her readings to task as you study the novels and their thematic concerns.

Morrison has attracted a great deal of critical attention and this section breaks down that work, suggesting particularly useful essays, or collections of essays, as well as indicating where you can find particular sorts of readings.

An excellent starting place for your critical reading is with texts that take a broad perspective, looking at a number of Morrison novels, and offering more than one critical perspective. For example, *Toni Morrison*, edited by Linden Peach, or *Toni Morrison*, by Jill Matus. The essays provide a clear introduction to thinking critically about these novels, each essay focusing upon a particular theme and novel.

However, as your analysis becomes more sophisticated you will want to look at more in-depth criticism, and this falls into a number of camps. There are a group of critics who focus primarily upon the idea of Morrison as a figurehead for the Black community in contemporary America. They critique her novels as representations of the community, and argue about the extent to which she is a good role model. This group is made up of critics like K. Sumana, in her work entitled *The Novels of Toni Morrison, A Study in Race, Gender and Class*, or Patrick Bryce Bjork's text *The Novels of Toni Morrison, the Search for Self and Place in the Community*.

Other critics focus on applying particular topics to Morrison's fiction. If, for example, you are particularly interested in looking at historical or geographical readings of these novels, then critics such as Wendy Harding and Jacky Martin discuss the clashing cultures at work in Morrison's fiction in *A World of Difference: An Inter-Cultural Study of Toni Morrison's Novels*. Or Darlene E. Erickson's essay 'The Black Search for Place in America' looks specifically at the setting of *Beloved* and talks about the importance of the geography of America and its history as partially slave-owning for novels such as *Beloved*.

If you want to test out different critical perspectives and get a feel for how different theories approach Morrison, start with an overview like that edited by Henry Louis Gates Jr. This offers a number of critical perspectives but it also, by including past as well as more current reading, gives you a sense of the development of ideas. Equally well thought-out and critically informative is Nancy Peterson's collection of essays entitled *Toni Morrison, Critical and Theoretical Approaches*, which outlines the approaches being taken, as well as providing interesting readings of the novels.

Equally, you may want to think about a particular kind of literary theory and discover how approaching a text with a distinct set of theoretical tools produces a different reading. In this case you could look, for example, at Philip Page's analysis of Morrison entitled *Dangerous Freedom, Fusion and Fragmentation in Toni Morrison's Novels*. This analysis focuses on Morrison's work as 'Postmodern'. Page examines ideas about fragmentation and separation, which are central concepts in identifying a text as being 'Postmodern'.

Morrison is a highly respected essayist as well as novelist, and as a teacher herself, she understands the importance of clarity in critical reading. Therefore, her own analysis of the texts she produces provides an excellent starting point for any engagement with criticism. However, she is also an immensely popular writer, and it is easy to become confused by the sheer quantity of Morrison criticism. This means that well-thought-out critical collections can be sophisticated but also negotiable entries into thinking about the author.

All works cited are listed in the Select Bibliography.

Glossary of literary terms

Allusion Where one text refers to another.

Ambivalence When your attitude to a person or an event is unresolved or unsure, perhaps because you feel both positive and negative about it.

Antithesis When two ideas are the direct opposite of one another; when two concepts embody values that contrast in every way. For example, the antithesis of peace is war.

Archetype Basic mythic formulas of plot or character.

Atrophy A withering, or drying up.

Binary opposition This is related to the idea of two concepts being opposed to one another, but the important factor here is that you have to understand both of the contrasting values in order to understand the opposition. For example, to understand the colour 'red' on a traffic light, you have to understand 'green'. If all lights were red there would be no opposition and the lights would mean nothing. Or if no one explained to you that red = STOP and green = GO, then the lights would make no sense.

Characterise To describe your understanding of a person, event or context. You pick particular terms that convey to a new reader what you consider to be the most important factors when observing your example. For instance, you might characterise Santa Claus as 'jolly and fat' or 'bearded and generous'.

Chronology The arrangement of dates and times in the order in which they occurred, to give you a sense of the sequence of events. This is particularly useful when novels are fragmented and the order of events is difficult to remember.

Circumscribe This literally means to draw a line around something, but here it suggests the events or ideas that surround or control a person or event. So you could say that a vicar is circumscribed by religious values.

Conceptualise To take your ideas and examples and explain them as a concept. You might talk about a rose as an object, and about the associations it has, such as Valentine's Day. You would conceptualise it by talking about the rose as representing the concept of 'love'.

Contextualise To take a set of events or individual characters and link them. By linking the disparate elements, you create a 'context' for the action or character. You might contextualise Beloved's death by linking and explaining the events that lead up to Sethe's decision to kill her.

Denouement Shorthand for the final solution in a play or novel. It is the crisis point at which the plot's twists and turns are explained to the audience. For example, the denouement of Shakespeare's *Othello* is Desdemona's murder and the explanation of Iago's trickery.

Emasculate/Emasculation This literally means to castrate or weaken, but here the sense is that masculinity is being undermined. It is to feminise a man, for example by suggesting that he is unmasculine because his female partner supports him or is more capable of doing his work than he is.

Empirical Basing an argument or opinion on facts or observations, as opposed to theories and ideas.

Empower To give an individual authority, licence or power – ideologically or thematically. For example, women are empowered by the right to vote as it gives them a 'voice' in the community and their views are represented.

Epitomise To encapsulate, or sum up, a complex idea in a word or phrase.

Extended metaphor A metaphor that runs throughout a paragraph or chapter, or even an entire novel. For instance, the metaphor of animalistic sex runs all through Iago's vocabulary in *Othello*; he constantly refers to the idea of Desdemona and Othello as coupling animals.

Genealogy The tracing of a family descent or history. It is another term for a family tree, although it is not necessarily mapped out as family trees are.

Historicise To locate an idea in a historical context. For example, to understand the particular events at 'Sweet Home' by discovering the events of slavery in order to comprehend the history to which the novel refers.

Holocaust This literally means 'burnt-offering', but it is employed in the context of the Second World War to mean 'a massive sacrifice or wholesale destruction'.

Impunity Exemption from punishment or injury: to be able to continue a particular course without any control, or rules attempting to control you.

Inscription A name that is written in a book to suggest ownership; the term is used here to suggest giving something meaning, just as a name is used to suggest belonging. For example, as children we often ascribe value to a particular toy or comforter as being the thing that gets us to sleep.

Ironise/Irony To express an idea by using a term that doesn't mean what it appears to say. When 'fish and chips' are described as top-class French *nouvelle cuisine*, the speaker is probably being ironic. Irony is also used to convey information to a particular audience and therefore excludes those who do not understand it.

Juxtapose To place two contrasting ideas, phrases or styles next to one another. A chapter may juxtapose characters or settings, for instance.

Modernist Applied to the group of writers and artists working around the time of the First World War whose work was characterised by experimentation with form.

Paradigm Where one thing becomes a measure or pattern for another.

Personification/Personified This has two meanings. 1) When an object or animal is given human characteristics – such as describing the sun's smile. 2) When a phrase or description sums up an attitude or set of ideas. For example, you could say that Sethe's attitude to Paul D is personified in Part One, Section 3 of *Beloved*.

Privileged This means highlighted or foregrounded – it places a particular idea, or set of ideas, at the forefront of the reader's mind.

Postmodern Characterised by an excessive self-consciousness, self aware literary experimentation, and a fragmentation of form.

Scoptophilic When an individual's attention is focused primarily through the eyes and is drawn predominantly by images or visual stimulus.

Semantic Focusing upon the relationship of language to meanings.

Stream of consciousness When a narrative is written to mirror the internal thought processes – the ideas that run through our minds even when we are apparently silent. It becomes a continual narrative.

Third-person narrator 'He' or 'She', as opposed to 'I'.

Transparent Something that is made clear or obvious.

Trilogy A set of three related works; it initially meant three Greek tragedies that were performed in quick succession. It is now taken to mean three texts that are all complete in their own right, but are connected thematically.

Trinity A group of three, or a union of three persons. However, it is usually understood to mean the Holy Trinity, the three parts of which are: God the Father (God), God the Son (Jesus) and God the Holy Spirit.

Biographical outline

1931 18 February: Chloe Anthony Wofford born in Lorain, Ohio, USA.

1949 Graduated from Lorain High School with honours. Began studying at Howard University. Changed first name to Toni.

1953 Graduated from Howard University with a Bachelor of Arts in English, and a minor in Classics.

1955 Graduated from Cornell University with a Master of Arts in American Literature. Took a teaching position at Texas Southern University.

1957 Took a teaching position at Howard University. Taught many future civil-rights leaders, including Stokely Carmichael, Andrew Young and author Claude Brown.

1964 Appointed Associate Editor at Random House textbooks in Syracuse, New York.

1967 Appointed Senior Editor at Random House in New York City.

1970 *The Bluest Eye* published.

1971 Appointed Associate Professor of English at the State University of New York at Purchase.

1973 *Sula* published.

1975 *Sula* nominated for the National Book Award for Fiction and received the Ohioana Book Award.

1976 Appointed a visiting lecturer at Yale University.

1977 *Song of Solomon* published. Appointed by President Carter to the

National Council on the Arts.

1978 Won the National Book Critics' Circle Award for Fiction and the American Academy and Institute of Arts and Letters Award for *Song of Solomon*.

1981 *Tar Baby* published. Appeared on the cover of the March edition of *Newsweek*. Became a member of the American Academy of Arts and Letters.

1983 Left editorial job at Random House.

1984 Appointed to the Albert Schweitzer Chair in the Humanities by the State University of New York in Albany.

1986 *Dreaming Emmett*, Morrison's first play, premiered in Albany at the Marketplace Theater.

1987 *Beloved* published. Won the New York State Governor's Arts Award, the first Washington College Literary Award, and was nominated for a National Book Award and a National Book Critics' Circle Award for *Beloved*.

1988 Won the Pulitzer Prize in fiction and the Robert F. Kennedy Award for *Beloved*.

1989 Named the Robert F. Goheen Professor in the Council of Humanities at Princeton University – the first black woman writer to hold a named chair at an Ivy League university. Won the Modern Language Association of America Commonwealth Award in Literature.

1990 Delivered the Clark Lectures at Trinity College, Cambridge University, and the Massey Lectures at Harvard University.

1992 *Jazz* published. *Playing in the Dark: Whiteness and the Literary Imagination* also published.

1993 Won the Nobel Prize for Literature.

1994 Appointed International Condorcet Chair at the Ecole Normale Supérieure and Collège de France. Won the Condorcet Medal and the Pearl Buck Award.

1996 Won the National Book Foundation Medal for Distinguished Contribution to American Letters.

1998 *Paradise* published. Film of *Beloved* released.

1999 *Paradise* shortlisted for the Orange Prize.
2000 Named a 2000 National Humanities Medalist.

Select bibliography

WORKS BY TONI MORRISON

FICTION
The Bluest Eye (Chatto and Windus, London 1979; Vintage, London, 1999)
Sula (Chatto and Windus, 1973; Vintage, 1988)
Song of Solomon (Chatto and Windus, 1978; Vintage, 1998)
Tar Baby (Chatto and Windus, 1981; Vintage, 1997)
Beloved (Chatto and Windus, 1987; Vintage, 1997)
Jazz (Chatto and Windus, 1992; Vintage, 2001)
Paradise (Chatto and Windus, 1998; Vintage, 1999)

CRITICAL WORKS
Birth of a Nation'hood: Gaze, Script and Spectacle in the O.J. Simpson Case (Vintage, 1997)
Race-ing Justice, En-gendering Power. Essays on Anita Hill, Clarence Thomas, and the Construction of Social Reality (Chatto, 1993)

INTERVIEWS AND SPEECHES
Conversations with Toni Morrison, ed. Danielle Guthrie-Taylor (University Press of Mississippi, Knoxville, 1994)
The Dancing Mind (Alfred Knopf, New York, 1997)

INTERVIEWS ON THE INTERNET

http://www.azer.com/aiweb/categories/magazine/63_folder/63_articles/63_morrison_nobel.html

This is a reproduction of Toni Morrison's acceptance speech on receiving the Nobel Prize for Literature

http://www.salon.com/audio/2000/10/05/morrison_paradise/

Morrison reading an excerpt from *Paradise*

http://dir.salon.com/books/int/1998/02/cov_si_02int.html

The Salon Interview – an extensive interview with the author

http://www.luminarium.org/contemporary/tonimorrison/toninter.htm

An excellent website offering a number of interviews, including one with the magazine *Time*.

BIOGRAPHICAL AND CRITICAL STUDIES

Patrick Bryce Bjork, *The Novels of Toni Morrison, the Search for Self and Place in the Community* (Peter Lang, New York, 1992)

J. Brooks Bouson, *Quiet as it's kept: Shame, Trauma, and Race in the novels of Toni Morrison* (University of New York Press, Albany, 2000)

Evelyn Brooks-Higginbothom (ed.), *The Harvard Guide to African American History* (Harvard University Press, Cambridge, Mass., 2001)

Marc C. Connor, *The Aesthetics of Toni Morrison, Speaking the Unspeakable* (University of Mississippi Press, Jackson, 2000)

Jan Furman, *Toni Morrison's Fiction* (University of South Carolina Press, Columbia, 1996)

Henry Louis Gates Jr (ed.), *Black Literature and Literary Theory* (Methuen, London, 1984)

Henry Louis Gates Jr and Anthony Appiah (eds), *Toni Morrison: Critical Perspectives Past and Present* (Amistad, New York, 1993)

Gurleen Grewal, *Circles of Sorrow, Lines of Struggle, the novels of Toni Morrison* (Louisiana State University Press, Baton Rouge, 1998)

Elizabeth Kella, *Beloved Communities* (Uppsala University Press, Uppsala, 2000)

Robert Lee (ed.), *Black Fiction, New Studies in the Afro-American Novel Since 1945* (Vision, London, 1980)

David Palumbo Liu, *The Ethnic Canon, Histories, Institutions and Interventions* (University of Minnesota Press, Minneapolis, 1995)

Wahneema Lubiano (ed.), *The House that Race Built, Original Essays by Toni Morrison, Angela Y. Davis, Cornel West and others on Black Americans and Politics in America Today* (Vintage, New York, 1998)

Jill Matus, *Toni Morrison* (Manchester University Press, Manchester, 1998)

David Middleton (ed.), *Toni Morrison's Fiction, Contemporary Criticism* (Garland Publishing Inc., New York, 1997)

Philip Page, *Dangerous Freedom, Fusion and Fragmentation in Toni Morrison's Novels* (University Press of Mississippi, Jackson, 1995)

Linden Peach (ed.), *Toni Morrison* (Macmillan, Basingstoke, 1998)

Nancy Peterson (ed.), *Toni Morrison, Critical and Theoretical Approaches* (Johns Hopkins University Press, Baltimore, 1997)

Carla Plasa (ed.), *Toni Morrison, Beloved* (Icon, Duxford, 1998)

Carla Plasa and Betty Ring (eds), *The Discourse of Slavery, Aphra Behn to Toni Morrison* (Routledge, London, 1994)

Saadi Simawe, *Black Orpheus, Music in African American Fiction from the Harlem Renaissance to Toni Morrison* (Garland, London, 2000)

K. Sumana, *The Novels of Toni Morrison, A Study in Race, Gender and Class* (Sangam Books, London, 1998)

Alladi Uma (ed.), *Toni Morrison, An Intricate Spectrum* (Arnold Associates, New Delhi, 1996)

The editors

Jonathan Noakes has taught English in secondary schools in Britain and Australia for fifteen years. For six years he ran A-level English studies at Eton College where he is a house-master.

Margaret Reynolds is Reader in English at Queen Mary, University of London, and the presenter of BBC Radio 4's *Adventures in Poetry*. Her publications include *The Sappho Companion* and (with Angela Leighton) *Victorian Women Poets*.

Louisa Joyner completed her PhD. at the University of London. She is an editor and critic.

Also available in Vintage

Toni Morrison

THE BLUEST EYE

'I imagine if our greatest American novelist William Faulkner were alive today he would herald Toni Morrison's emergence as a kindred spirit . . . Discovering a writer like Toni Morrison is the rarest of pleasures'
Washington Post

'*The Bluest Eye* is an enquiry into the reasons why beauty gets wasted in this country. The beauty in this case is black; the wasting is done by a cultural engine that seems to have been designed to murder possibilities . . . and she does it with a prose so precise, so faithful to speech and so charged with pain and wonder that the novel becomes poetry'
New York Times

'*The Bluest Eye* is a fine book, a lament for all starved and stunted children everywhere'
Daily Telegraph

'Morrison's style rivets the reader . . . her synaesthetic, often rhythmic, even chanting prose recalls both Faulkner and Emily Dickinson'
Times Literary Supplement

VINTAGE

ALSO AVAILABLE IN VINTAGE LIVING TEXTS

❏	*Martin Amis*	0099437651	£6.99
❏	*Margaret Atwood*	009943704X	£6.99
❏	*Louis de Bernières*	0099437570	£6.99
❏	*Sebastian Faulks*	0099437562	£6.99
❏	*Ian McEwan*	0099437554	£6.99
❏	*Toni Morrison*	009943766X	£6.99
❏	*Salman Rushdie*	0099437643	£6.99
❏	*Jeanette Winterson*	0099437678	£6.99

- All Vintage books are available through mail order or from your local bookshop.
- Payment may be made using Access, Visa, Mastercard, Diners Club, Switch and Amex, or cheque, eurocheque and postal order (sterling only).

❏❏❏❏❏❏❏❏❏❏❏❏❏❏❏❏

Expiry Date:_____ Signature:_____

Please allow £2.50 for post and packing for the first book and £1.00 per book thereafter.

ALL ORDERS TO:
Vintage Books, Books by Post, TBS Limited, The Book Service,
Colchester Road, Frating Green, Colchester, Essex, CO7 7DW, UK.
Telephone: (01206) 256 000
Fax: (01206) 255 914

NAME: _____
ADDRESS: _____
_____
_____

Please allow 28 days for delivery. Please tick box if you do not wish to receive any additional information.   ❏
Prices and availability subject to change without notice.